STAR MANA

STAR MANA

The Healing Energies
of Hawaii

KEN CARLSON

STARMEN PRESS
KILAUEA, HAWAII

Published by: Starmen Press
PO Box 698
Kilauea, HI 96754

Executive editor: Ellen Kleiner
Editor: Ann Mason
Book design and typography: Richard Harris
Cover design and production: Janice St. Marie
Interior illustration: Chris Carlson
Back cover photo: Elizabeth Pianka

A Blessingway book

Preassigned Library of Congress Catalog Card Number: 97-92525

ISBN 0-9659716-0-0

Printed in the United States of America on acid-free recycled paper

10 9 8 7 6 5 4 3 2 1

To Chris and Roger
with thanks for your support

I am grateful to all those who have supported the evolution of this book. I am grateful that we are literate in a world in which 70 percent of the people can't read. For these blessings and many more, I thank God.

C O N T E N T S

F O R E W O R D

How wonderful it is to have available to us spiritual medicine that has the power to balance, heal, and align the mental, emotional, and spiritual levels of our being. Because these more subtle aspects of our being often go unrecognized and untreated, the whole person is usually not taken into consideration. Frequently it is the troubled emotions, old negative mental programs, or soul-level imbalances that manifest in the physical body as dis-ease. By using flower essences, gem essences, or a combination of the two, the vibrational frequencies of the mental, emotional, and spiritual levels of the individual are gently and successfully attended to. In this way, the root cause of dis-ease is remedied and a much fuller state of health results.

I am very grateful to Ken Carlson for writing this book and to him and his partner, Roger Denisewicz, for having the insight, attunement, and love in their hearts to create these remedies. With their integrity and the nurturing healing energy of Kauai, I know that these elixirs will find their way into the hearts and homes of people everywhere to provide support and powerful healing energy in a safe, gentle, and effective way.

Katrina Raphaell
Author of *Crystal Enlightenment, Crystal Healing,*
and *The Crystalline Transmission*

P R E F A C E

The title of this book, *Star Mana,* symbolizes the synergistic creation of energy. This phenomenon begins with the sun, which has an energizing effect on all living things. When it shines on the morning dew that forms on plants, it causes the vibrational energies of these plants to rise into the water. The sun is our star, and in Hawaii the energy of the plant is called *mana,* a term meaning life force that is discussed in several sections of this book.

Star Mana first describes my life path and the effects the healing energies of Hawaii have had on me. It was the influence of Hawaii, and specifically Kauai, that inspired me to create new Hawaiian flower essences and then combine them with gem essences. This magical island has opened doors to a new career and has sparked a desire to offer others the healing knowledge and tools I have discovered. I bless this place and give thanks for how it has blessed me.

Other chapters of this book discuss our divine nature and how it is related to profound levels of healing untapped by Western medicine; ancient Hawaiian healing techniques and modern research on them; past and current research on the energy of plants and homeopathic medicine; the uses of flower and gem essences; and how to work with these essences individually as well as in combination.

The tools introduced in this book are meant to empower individuals to take control of their physical and emotional conditions rather than seeing themselves as victims of circumstance. Although these tools and insights are not a substitute for regular medical attention or a cure for all conditions, they can be effective aids in living a more conscious, healthy, and loving life free from emotional and physical dysfunction. It is my hope that they will have a healing and awakening influence.

1

STARMAN AWAKENS

My life began outside of Boston, an area of the country where people pride themselves on doing things properly, which usually means the way they have always been done. If we assume that our forefathers had everything figured out, then repeating the wisdom of the past makes good sense. By the time I finished college in the 1960s, however, I no longer believed that everything had been figured out, and I was not interested in doing anything the way it had been done before. I began to break out of old patterns and try different ways of experiencing life.

After college, I went off to California in search of the life the Beachboys were singing about. To my great delight, I found it. Although I was mixed up and actually rebelling more than embracing new ideas, it was just the jump-start I needed for a new lease on life. Then, unconsciously hoping to earn my father's respect, I went to law school for four years while I worked full-time, ultimately passing the California and Utah bar exams. I soon noticed, however, that my lawyer friends were turning into callous robots after they began practicing law, and once again I rebelled, refusing to allow that dehumanizing process to consume me as well. Instead of practicing law, I moved to Salt Lake City, Utah, where I purchased and ran a small factory, hoping this line of work would be satisfying as well as successful.

One day in the middle of winter, while I was under a mobile home installing aluminum panels, my lofty ideas were overwhelmed by physical realities. My hands were frozen and bleeding; my business was going down the tubes; and I began wondering how I was going to rise above the cold and muddy pit I was in. The extremes of cold and pain must have broken through the combination of my New England traditional thinking and my rebelliousness, because it suddenly became clear that life would be easier and warmer if I worked inside an office somewhere doing what I was trained to do. Consequently, in an attempt to reconcile my ideals with my concerns about being a traditional lawyer, I joined Legal Aid.

Helping poor people in obvious need was deeply rewarding. Eventually, I went back to California to establish a private practice, all the while determined not to practice law the way the profession was being modeled. I opened an office in the Bay Area and began figuring out how to survive economically and still dedicate as much time as possible to helping disadvantaged people.

At the time, my lifestyle was simple. I lived communally in Berkeley on a total of $250 a month, and thus did not have to compromise my beliefs by accepting all kinds of clients to pay the bills. Instead, I had the flexibility to pursue only the cases and causes most compelling to me. My love of the land, along with my perception that the earth and its people were being poisoned, led me to focus exclusively on environmental litigation.

Life took on new meaning for me as I fought the bad guys and helped redistribute the wealth among their victims. The questionable activities of some major American drug, chemical, and asbestos companies fueled my quest to right their wrongs. Their obsession with profits had motivated them to cover up the adverse health effects caused by their products. So engrossed did I become in this mission that I was unaware of the subtle toll it was taking. Working day in and day out in the system, I eventually realized, had ensnared me in the same predicament I had escaped from at least twice before. Although this time the conditions, the cause, and the money were all good, my life force was again being sucked out of me.

Then in 1981, I experienced the healing energies of Hawaii for the second time in my life. The effects were so wonderful that I returned to Hanalei Bay, on the north shore of Kauai, with my wife, Chris, and daughter, Preeta, two or three times a year for the next five years. Finally, in 1986 I walked out of my California law office forever and made Kauai my permanent home.

We bought some land, built a house, and had a second daughter, Ariel. My strife seemed miles behind me. But as we settled into life in paradise, the healing energies of Kauai began to work on me in unexpected ways. Whereas my career and busy big-city life had previously caused me to feel special, I suddenly could no longer judge my self-worth by what others reflected back to me. As I began examining my actions and motivations, it became embarrassingly clear that I had been acting out patterns of behavior and fighting to protect ideas and lifestyles that had nothing to do with who I really was.

We purposefully lived without television, and the remoteness of Kauai left me with few distractions to cover up the pain and confusion festering beneath the surface of my consciousness. Meditation, swimming, and surfing were great, but they did not pay the bills and provided only a temporary respite from the issues emerging from within me.

Soon, my passion for rescuing the victim from the jaws of the dragon drove me back into the legal arena. On the island of Hawaii, the state of Hawaii and various companies had been testing the idea of drilling deep into the Kilauea volcano and capturing the heat and energy to produce electricity. The idea seemed viable when viewed through the eyes of those who would benefit from selling electricity. Geothermal power had been successfully produced in many locations, and those behind the project were hoping it would work in Hawaii as well.

Although many Native Hawaiians and local residents warned the developers that the goddess Pele would be angered by this invasion of her belly, the project went forward. The location of the power plant—just three hundred feet from a residential neighborhood—was an invitation to disaster, and eventually, toxic gases vented into nearby residences and into the school buses that loaded outside the gates of the facility. A new developer took over, promising that the errors of the past would not be repeated, but the promise was short-lived. In 1991 the drilling rig, boring into the hottest geothermal resource on earth, blew out, resulting in mass evacuations as well as respiratory and central nervous system damage to people living around the plant. As a result, I spent the next six years litigating to shut down the project and compensate the victims.

Another cause that attracted me was the plight of Native Hawaiians. Hundreds of years before, New Englanders like me had come to Hawaii to "save the native people from their evil ways." The outsiders proceeded to get rich off the land, strip the Hawaiian people of their religious and cultural foundations, and finally, overthrow the ruling monarchy. In 1921 the United States Congress, in an attempt to make partial amends, enacted legislation to put Hawaiians back onto the land by leasing them tracts at the rate of one dollar for ninety-nine years. However, the amount of land set aside for these "Hawaiian Homelands"—200,000 acres throughout all the Hawaiian Islands—was insufficient to meet the needs of the people. And the government agency set up to administer the land became so preoccupied with running the Hawaiian Homelands program for the state that it ignored the tens of thousands of Native Hawaiians on the waiting list for land.

In a semiconscious act of payback for the actions of my fellow New Englanders who had created the problem, I decided to help rectify the Native Hawaiians' plight. Through a series of lawsuits, I attempted to get Native Hawaiians onto the land rather than let them die on the waiting list. Working with Native Hawaiians added new insight to my limited knowledge of their culture, their love of the land, and their religious roots.

To remain balanced during these exhausting legal struggles, I rooted myself in the land, arranging my daily routine so I could spend an hour working with the land for every hour spent in my head. The earth had a supernatural grounding influence on me. Adhering to this regime, I eventually cultivated an orchard of over one hundred fruit trees as well as gardens of flowers and vegetables, all the while acquiring a greater appreciation of nature's vitality.

I also worked with psychotherapy, meditation, the Hawaiian philosophy of *huna* and shamanic practices, breath work, network chiropractic, and flower essences. This work, combined with the energy of Kauai, played a significant role in my recovery from decades of confusion and compromise.

Five years ago I began to have a more intense relationship with the energy of my orchard and gardens. One day while lying on the ground among the fruit trees, I psychically reached out to their energy, or spirit, and was almost immediately filled with a beautiful pale blue light. I received answers to my questions about how, who, and why, and the spirit of the orchard offered its help in maintaining the health and welfare of individual fruit trees. Soon afterward, the trees began growing vigorously and became more resistant than ever before to pest infestations.

A short time later, while standing in my gardens one afternoon, I experienced an even more unusual phenomenon. I had allowed many of the vegetables to go to flower and seed, and what had once been a simple vegetable garden looked more like a beautiful flower garden. Suddenly a higher consciousness filled my mind and I was looking down on the flowers, seeing them as energy fuel. I was observing the plants not as I had before, but with a heightened perception, as if from a cosmic perspective.

With this new way of seeing, I began testing the effects on my well-being of flower after flower, first in my gardens and later all over the island. Guided by an inspiration that seemed to be coming from the flowers themselves, I began collecting unique blossoms that were growing in and around the wettest place on earth and using them to create flower essences. The mountain flowers seemed to have different qualities from those growing near the seashore. The colors and shapes of the flowers became increasingly more significant to me the more I experimented with them and noted certain correlations.

Eventually, my knowledge of flowers and their healing

properties grew to the point where I was using these Kauai flower essences to treat a wide variety of conditions. Although I had used commercial flower essences to balance my emotional states for more than fifteen years, the Kauai flower essences began playing a more important role in my mental and physical health.

My life was inextricably altered by my new view of flowers as a means for healing and for revitalizing energy. Something—caused either by the use of flower essences or by my more cosmic perspective—was propelling me deeper and deeper into my own healing process, as well as planetary healing.

As time passed, it became harder for me to continue practicing law. Although I still felt compassion for those I was trying to assist, I could no longer identify the other side as the enemy. As I began to more fully comprehend the notion that we help create whatever happens to us, good or bad, the roles of victim and victimizer became intertwined. While not denying the effects of others, I saw that each of us also plays a part, consciously or unconsciously, in our life's drama, even though we often refuse to see the effects of our actions, both in our own lives and in the lives of others.

My new cosmic perspective was further enhanced one day a few years ago as I was standing in court responding to a judge. A white light suddenly appeared around his head, then grew so prominent that, in my amazement, I forgot what I was saying. I have experienced similar distractions upon viewing other people's auras in various settings. Although it may seem such occurrences would help me see the metaphysical side of the law, in practice they prevented me from focusing on the adversarial nature of the legal system—not usually an advantageous mind-set from the perspective of winning legal battles.

During one lengthy set of cases in front of the same judge, my inability to perceive the adversarial nature of legal proceedings actually proved useful. The judge—no longer perceived subconsciously as my father sitting above me and judging me for my failures and errors—appeared as a friendly man with a big white halo shining around his head. Even more amazingly, the instant I began perceiving him differently, his attitude toward me and my clients improved. In the end, with his help, the cases were settled out of court.

Although the legal profession has been a valuable teacher for many years, I have become increasingly aware that it operates out of the lower vibrational energies of fear and anger. And since I believe I deserve to be surrounded by higher dimensional frequencies, I have finally decided not to practice law any longer and to walk away from an immersion that is holding me back. Joseph Campbell called such a choice "following your bliss."

With my new expanded perception, I have begun receiving information from other energies, or entities. One important vision was revealed to me several years ago during a network chiropractic session with a gifted healer, Michael McBride. In this vision I saw that Kauai is the northernmost tip of the old lost continent of Lemuria. The people living on Lemuria twenty-five thousand years ago were closely united with their true spirit identities, making negative emotions like fear, guilt, and anger practically nonexistent in their civilization. In addition, their bodies were not as dense as ours are today.

I discovered that Lemurians used flowers to elevate the subtle energy that drew them away from their spiritual centers and into the denser realm of thoughts. They also bred flowers to create flower essences that would respond to their emotional and physical needs. After cataclysmic earth changes, Lemuria was covered by the Pacific Ocean, and all that is left of it are the peaks that we identify as Kauai (on the north) and the Easter Islands (on the south).

In the vision I was asked to find flowers from tenacious weeds and vines, and make essences from them. These potent essences, I was told, would help people reach the higher energy frequencies experienced by the Lemurians. So significant was this vision that I was determined not only to discover the appropriate flowers but to make the essences available to others and to share my knowledge.

Since I began making flower essences, I have experienced profound personal healing from my exposure to their sacred energies. These energies have significantly altered my self-perception as well. I see myself no longer as an individual beset by limitation, but rather as a person who comes from the stars on a long path of awakening to the reality that I have no limitations! As a result of my changed perceptions, several of my friends began calling me "Starman," a name I have reluctantly accepted, for I sincerely believe that I have lived on many planets in numerous star systems over countless lifetimes. This is probably true for most of us—we are Beings from the stars, living on earth.

I remain connected with my soul, or higher self, through focused prayer. The practice of prayer reminds me that the role I am playing as a conduit for the sacred energies of the cosmos brings about the same physical and emotional healing in me as others experience when they take the Kauai essences. For this, I am deeply grateful to each and every deva and guide that works with me.

THE TRUE NATURE OF HEALING

hat is healing? Is it only curing disease or is it something far more profound? The answer is different for everyone. For many people, life consists of actively coping with events as they unfold. If that coping is accomplished adequately, they feel okay. For other people, there is more to life than just coping.

Let us consider the possibility that at one point in time, all individuals were merged with a reality so pure and beautiful that being away from it for even a moment brought tears of longing to return to this natural state of effortless joy and peace. Now, remember the moments of pure joy you have experienced in your life, either as a child or as an adult, and acknowledge that those experiences were real and wonderful. Repeat this exercise several times a day. By accessing your memory of how beautiful your experiences have been and of the effortless joy and peace you have known, you are less likely to be drawn into the consensus reality of believing that just coping is enough.

On one level, healing is often rather simple. Drugs are available to block pain, dull the perception of depression, kill the bugs residing in the body, and stimulate pleasure. High-tech medicine can clear blocked arteries, transplant organs, replace worn-out joints, and track DNA sequencing. The only prerequisite to healing via these modalities is having adequate medical insurance.

The wonders of modern medicine, however, can only bring about healing on a superficial level, maintaining the status quo. A deeper level of healing needs to take place after you return home from the doctor's office. This type of healing requires transmuting the pain of longing for love and union, a pain so deep and profound that we usually deny its existence. The first step in activating this form of healing is to break out of consensus reality and believe that it is possible to live a loving, joy-filled life. In fact, such a life is not only possible, it is our natural condition.

If feeling love and joy is our natural condition, then how did we deviate so far from this state? Some people maintain that a diabolical force drags humanity down, and that feelings of joy and love can be experienced only in the afterlife. I have found that this belief in a dark force permeates our world because of a lack of understanding of the law of cause and effect which, as a variation on the Golden Rule, states that the harm we do unto others comes back to haunt us. In our confusion, we are willing to entertain any crazy idea that might otherwise explain the cause of the pain and suffering we see around us. Although the truth about the divine nature of reality has been known for a long time, the fact that we create our own reality within a divine framework is unfortunately not sensational or newsworthy enough to capture our attention.

To gain some perspective on how our lives have become so confusing, it is helpful to remember the circumstances of your birth. Many people are able to access these memories through rebirthing, holotropic breath work, and other methods designed to help us undo the damaging effects of the birthing process. If these memories are presently unavailable to you, imagine that you are a peaceful baby inside your mother's womb, and all is well. The temperature is perfect; the gentle rocking is soothing and comforting; you are telepathically connected to your mother's love for you. As the pregnancy progresses, however, your mother has fearful thoughts—about the life-threatening prospects of childbirth, or the possibility of having to endure great pain in labor—all of which are communicated to you. Eventually, your new home becomes more limiting because of these constricting thoughts and stress until, at the time of birth, your world is in upheaval and you are experiencing a thrashing, undulating reality. Muscle spasms force you into a tight, compressed tunnel where, as the pressure mounts, your mother's tension and pain add to your own discomfort and apprehension.

Suddenly, your head breaks out of the darkness, and your tiny body emerges gasping for air because the umbilical cord is wrapped tightly around your neck. Finally, after strange hands loosen the cord, air enters your lungs. You are then thrust under a glaring light, shaking and shivering, filled with new sensations. For the first time your skin feels like an envelope, a limiting boundary as you struggle to comprehend where you are and what is happening. Your mother is allowed to hold you for a few brief moments before you are taken away, washed with water that feels too cold, and placed in a plastic box. In short, you have moved from a place of nurturing and love to one of pain and struggle, and at last to abandonment.

Because the nervous system of the fetus is formed early on, it is fully functioning and ready to imprint the traumas of birth. Fear of pain and death, fear of suffocation, stress associated with the upheaval of the birth, and feelings of rejection all become recorded. These traumas push the newborn into overload, eclipsing many of his ongoing experiences. The nervous system then processes these experiences into a network through which all future perception is filtered. As a result, the child's views of life will be heavily colored by his birth experiences.

The period of infancy through adolescence usually adds more emotional traumas to the nervous system. When the time arrives for the individual to assert his independence, his identity is repeatedly short-circuited by feelings that have no rational relationship to events going on at the moment. Having lost all memory of his divine nature, the individual creates a new sense of identity based on feedback from family and society.

This is not a farfetched scenario; it is the story of nearly every birth process, including my own. From the perspective of the individual who sees through a veil of unconscious, fearful, and traumatic events, there is much to heal. It is in these areas that more profound healing must occur for us to return to our natural state of joy. Healing on this level entails going behind the network of events recorded in the nervous system and reexperiencing our divine nature.

To do this, we must dissociate from all forms of self-identification that hinge on how good we look, how smart we are, and other types of feedback from those around us. We must also detach from fixed parameters established by the political and religious systems into which we were born, particularly the transmitted definitions of "good" and "bad," as well as the message that we are sinners before God.

Identifying with the ideas promoted by personal feedback and politico-religious dogma reaps rewards when actions are consistent with consensus reality, but causes despair when they are not. Only by disengaging from these trauma-based dilemmas can we discover a more accurate form of self-identification.

My own long search for my true self has guided me into many domains of healing. Those that have proved most helpful come under the category of vibrational medicine, which is based on quantum physics. Quantum physicists have shown that at the particle level all matter is vibrating energy. We, in other words, are pure energy that has been strongly influenced by our life experiences, resulting in loss of memory concerning our true nature. Healing, then, entails dissociating from energies that do not reflect our genuine nature and returning to our true resonance.

All energy has a vibration. Methods of vibrational healing such as prayer, chanting, and the laying on of hands have been practiced for centuries by Hawaiians, as well as many other indigenous peoples. Other ancient energetic approaches to healing include acupuncture and Vedic medicine. Radionics, dowsing, kinesiology, flower essences, gem essences, and color therapy have emerged in this century. Although scientists have verified the effectiveness of all these methods, practitioners of allopathic medicine persist in viewing the individual as a system of wires and plumbing.

Before arriving at the point of needing an electrician or a plumber to fix our ailing bodies, we can begin to reverse the damaging effects of believing that we are less than divine. Among the many paths that lead in this direction are those nourished by the healing energies of Hawaii, with its tropical sun, negative ions from the ocean and the rain, verdantly lush green vegetation, ancient force fields held in the land, and aloha spirit. Although it is helpful to experience these energies directly, it is also possible to benefit from them through a variety of vibrational tools, including Hawaiian flower and gem essences. Such tools have the power to heal us on many levels.

HAWAIIAN
HEALING METHODS

P rior to the arrival of missionaries bearing Christian
teachings in the 1800s, healing in Hawaii was based
on an intuitive understanding of the energy of sick-
ness. Much of this understanding was rooted in the *huna*
philosophy of ancient Polynesian healers, which Hawaiian
author and shaman Serge Kahili King summarizes in the following seven principles: The world is what you think it is;
there are no limits; energy flows where attention goes; now
is the moment of power; to love is to be happy with; all
power comes from within; and effectiveness is the measure
of truth.[1]

Hawaiians encountered by the missionaries had a remarkably sophisticated knowledge of human anatomy and of the
curative uses of plants. Many of these healing methods are
still in use.

P R A Y E R

The core of Hawaiian healing was, and still is, prayer (*pule*). The *pule* is not just for healing; it is also a required beginning to any significant event, such as a legislative session, hula gathering, or community meeting. Although the deity to which one prays may vary, the consciousness remains the same. It must be *pono,* which means "right," or "proper." And the person praying must be respectful, use correct procedures, and be precise to effectively transmit the prayer.

Early Hawaiians divided disease into two classifications: those caused by forces outside the body and those caused by forces within. In both instances, prayer was used to seek relief from an illness. Master healers known as *kahunas* administered their individual healing techniques, all of which included prayer. The *kahuna 'ana'ana* (practitioner of black magic) performed his work exclusively through prayer, whereas the *kahuna lapa'au* (medical doctor) and the *kahuna la'au lapa'au* (herbalist) offered prayers to accompany their medications and treatment.[2]

The magical powers evoked by the prayers of *kahunas* were investigated and recorded by several of the missionary scholars who came to the Hawaiian Islands. Later, in the 1940s and 1950s, psychoreligious researcher and author Max Freedom Long studied how *kahunas* prayed. He found that they held in their minds a clear image of the requested outcome. Next, with strong faith, they produced and held a charge of *mana,* the life force. Finally, they visualized the lower self sending the request on a flow of *mana* up to the higher self. This prayer was said with a strong, clear voice (*ka leo*) and usually, for maximum effectiveness, was repeated three times.[3]

Long regarded the advice of Dr. William Brigham—who

spent forty years as curator for the Bishop Museum in Honolulu and recorded the performance of miracles by *kahunas*—as the foundation for his further studies. Dr. Brigham's advice: "Always keep watch for three things in the study of this magic. There must be some form of consciousness in back of and directing the process of magic. There must also be some form of force used in exerting this control, if we can but recognize it. And last, there must be some form of substance, visible or invisible, through which the force can act. Watch always for these, and if you can find any one, it may lead to the others."[4]

David K. Bray, a modern-day *kahuna,* describes the force used in prayers as *mana:* "The *mana* was received from heaven through prayer. A man prayed constantly and made daily offerings to his own *aumakua,* a spiritual guardian spirit, generally an ancestor. The *aumakua,* being in heaven, listened to his child on earth and interceded with the great god for this divine spirit. It was as though heaven were a reservoir of spiritual power, and that power descended to the *kahuna* on earth through the *aumakua.* The more the *kahuna* prayed, the more spiritual power he received, until his person was like a small reservoir of spiritual power."[5]

There was great diversity among those who worshipped deities in ancient Hawaii, because individuals had different gods. Women usually worshipped various female deities such as Hina, Pele, Hi'iaka, and Laka, whereas men worshipped a pantheon of male deities. The male deities, worshipped by everyone from chiefs to common people, were Ku, Kane, Kanaloa, and Lono.[6]

Ku, the first of the great gods to arrive, was the protector of all of Hawaii—its island kingdoms as well as individual families. One of the many prayers to Ku is as follows:

E Ku I ka lana mai nuu!	O god Ku, of the sacred altar!
E Ku I ka ohia lele!	O Ku of the scaffolding of the *ohia* tree!
E Ku I ka ohia-lehua!	O Ku carved of the *ohia-lehua!*
E Ku I ka ohia-ha uli!	O Ku of the flourishing *ohia-ha!*
E Ku I ka ohia moewai!	O Ku of the water-seasoned *ohia* tree!
E Ku mai ka lani!	O Ku, come down from heaven!
Ku I ke ao!	O Ku, god of light!
E Ku I ka honua!	O Ku, ruler of the world!
E ka ohia ihi!	O magnificent *ohia* tree!
E Ku I ka lani-ka-ohia, ka haku-ohia!	O Ku of the *ohia* tree carved by a king, lord of *ohia* gods!
A ku, a lele, ua noa.	It lifts, it flies, it is gone.
A noa ia K'u.	The tabu is removed by Ku.
Ua uhi kapa mahana,	Robed are we in warm *tapa,*
Hoomahanahana heiau,	A warmth that relaxes the rigors of the *heiau,*
E noa! E noa!	Freedom! Freedom!
Amama wale! Ua noa!	The load is lifted! There is freedom![7]

Kane, the next of the powerful gods, is said to have created numerous springs around the islands as he struck the rocks with his *kauila* (staff). Following is one of the prayers to Kane:

Ka wai laahia, e Kane-i-ka-wai.	The sacred water, O Kane-of-the-water.
Ka wai la ia, e Kane.	It is the water of Kane.
Ka wai I ka hikina, e Kane	The water in the east, O Kane.
Nou Ka Wai Koo-lihilhil.	Yours is the water in the long gourd gushing forth.

Kulia o lau mahu'e luna,   Position of leaves wide open
o lau meha.   above, lone leaves.
O na meha huli honua.   Lone leaves that face the earth.
Hoouka kai hoe, e Kane,   Put your paddle inside, O Kane,
A holo, e Kane, a kele,   And go, O Kane, and sail away,
e Kane,   O Kane,
He kaua ka lua kaala hoku,   A war is the pit for sling stone stars,
A hopu I ke aka, I ke aka   And hold the reflection, the
o Kane.   reflection of Kane.
A kolo, I kolo a'e, kolo   And move gently along, move
anunue,   the rainbow,
E ukuhi I ka wai   Pour out the water
Pakahi ka lau no'ena'e,   One by one the leaves, the frag-
ka lau 'ala o ka nahele.   rant leaves of the woodland.
Kihikihi oo ia   Projecting at angles
Keekeehi iho no oe I ka   Tread firmly to the east.
hikina.
Owai ia alii o ka hikina?   Who is the chief of the east?
O Kane alii oe la, o no Uli.   You are chief Kane, of the Uli
    line.

Au'au I ka wai ponihiwa,   Bathe in the dark waters of
e kane,   Kane,
He aka-ku kau I ka   A vision placed on the top of
manawa,   the head,
Ku mai a'e la ipu hele,   Caused the traveling gourd to
e Kane.   land, O Kane.
Ina ke oho o Mano Ka   Here the hair of Mano is going,
hele ana, e Kane,   O Kane,
I ke ala kaua'i akua,   In the way of the footprint of
kapau'i no Hina.   deity, footprint of Hina.
Eia ka pule, eia ke   Here is the prayer, here is the
kanaenae nou,   chant of eulogy for you,
e Kane ke akua.   O Kane the deity.[8]

The god Kanaloa reportedly came to Hawaii with Kane. Individuals treating the sick often appeal to Kanaloa in prayers such as the following:

E Kanaloa, ke akua ka hee!	O Kanaloa, god of the squid!
Eia kau mai o (inoa).	Here is your patient (name).
E ka hee o kai uli,	O squid of the deep blue sea,
Ka hee o ka lua one,	Squid that inhabits the coral reef,
Ka hee i ka papa,	Squid that burrows in the sand,
Ka hee pio!	Squid that squirts water from its sack!
Eia ka oukou mai,	Here is a sick man for you to
o (inoa),	heal (name),
He mai hoomoe ia no ka	A patient put to bed for treat-
hee palaha.	ment by the squid that lies flat.[9]

The message of this prayer is that the disease will slip off of the sick person like a squid. Indeed, after the treatment, a fisherman is sent out to catch a squid.

The fourth god, Lono, was the patron of land fertility and of the *kahuna la'au lapa'au,* or herbal doctor. In the latter form, he is associated with many healing plants.[10]

In addition to the four major gods were the *aumakuas,* personal guardians of individuals and their families. Common *aumakuas* included lizards and sharks.[11] One such lizard was the *mo'o,* a thirty-foot-long black reptile that lived in fishponds. The shark was the ultimate symbol of strength, daring, and courage; stories are told of family members imperiled at sea who were saved by their *aumakua* shark.[12]

Aumakuas were intimate members of the family and were appealed to for healing, guidance, and before feasting, with prayers such as the following:

E na 'aumakua mai ka pa'a iluna ka pa'a ilalo,	O guardians from the solid above to the solid below,
Ka hoohu'io a me ka halawai,	From the zenith to the horizon,
E ka 'ai, he 'awa.	Here is the food and the *'awa*.
'E 'ike ia'u ia (inoa) ka 'oukou pulapula.	Take notice of me (name), your offspring.
O ke ola mau loa no ko'u a kau I ka pua'aneane,	Let my life continue till I reach extreme old age,
A kanikoo, a haumaka 'iole	Until the cane sounds (and I am)
Kolopupu, a haumaka 'iole.	Bent with age, and blurred eyes of a rat.
O ke ola ia a 'oukou, e na' 'aumakua	It is life by you, O *'aumakua*
Amama, ua noa, lele wale.	*'Amama*, free of tabu, flown away.[13]

The people of Old Hawaii also had a third category of gods, the *kapuas*. Less powerful than the four great gods and the *aumakuas*, they were included in most prayers in an indirect way.

Although all humans were said to have *mana*, the largest supply of this life force came from the deities. Praying well and often was the best way to build a reserve of *mana* that could be used for healing. This energy was also passed by a *kahuna* to the successor sharing the *kahuna's* last breath.

It is evident to me that when personal *mana* is focused, it is a powerful healing force. At night before bed, when my body prepares to go into a healing mode, I build up my *mana* and tell my body to correct whatever condition needs attention. This technique can even be effective for health issues that are considered genetic. All that is needed is *mana,* focus, and clear instructions to the body or subconscious mind.

One of the ancient Hawaiians' most unusual uses of prayer for healing was in response to an adversary's death prayers (*na pule 'ana 'ana*). So powerful were the forces created from prayer that they were sometimes used to kill or injure enemies. A special class of *kahunas* known as *kahuna ho' opi' opi'o* were trained specifically to counteract this type of evil sorcery. Their prayers were used to turn the effect of the death spell back on the individual who sent it. A simple version of such a prayer is *"Ho'i no'ai I kou kahu"* ("Go back and destroy your keeper").[14]

In the past, Hawaiians were skilled at using prayer for healing. They activated the power of prayer with their voices (*ka leo*), believing that the sound vibration of the voice created an energy resonance that could be used to heal or kill. Today, Hawaiians gifted with the ability to chant still have a strong effect on those who hear their voices. Like many people, I have felt the authority, strength, and power of the chanted words, even though I do not understand them.

The power of words uttered in ancient languages is widely acknowledged by present-day Tibetan Buddhists and Jews, who continue to use Sanskrit and ancient Hebrew in their mantras and prayers. In this regard, it is interesting to speculate that the Catholic Church may have lost some of its power when it stopped using the original Latin in the Mass.

The importance of sound in creating a desired outcome is beautifully stated by the Apostle John: "In the beginning was the Word, and the Word was with God, and the Word was God. . . . And the Word was made flesh and dwelt among us."[15] The creative potential of the clearly focused spoken word is also captured in the creation story in

Genesis: "Let there be light. . . . Let the waters under the heaven be gathered together unto one place, and let dry *land* appear: and it was so."[16] The palpable power of Hawaiian chants and the historical precedent of using the spoken word to produce a desired result provide a good incentive to employ spoken prayer often in our lives.

L A Y I N G   O N   O F   H A N D S

Another ancient healing method used by *kahunas* was laying hands on the patient, since touching was the best way to transfer *mana*. Many traditional Hawaiian stories and legends include healing rituals that end with the laying on of hands. Max Freedom Long reported that *kahunas* accumulated high charges of *mana,* visualized a picture of the healed condition, presented the picture to their higher self, and then laid their hands on the patient while *mana* was transferred.[17] This practice has been carried out in Hawaii for centuries.

W A T E R

Water, too, was a carrier of *mana*. In fact water, according to Max Freedom Long and Serge Kahili King, is a symbol for *mana* in the *huna* philosophy. In *huna,* freshwater was not merely a physical life-giving element; it also had a spiritual quality. The phrase "Water of Life of Kane" is frequently repeated in prayers of thanks and invocations used in offering fruits of the land, in prayers chanted while planting, and in prayers for rain. Moreover, all four of the major gods are included in prayers that speak of the "water of life."[18]

Freshwater was also used in purification rituals for people and for such places as a *heiau* (place of worship) or family altar. The symbolic act of being purified with water predates by many centuries the baptisms used for cleansing people from sin. Whereas baptism by immersion was a symbolic use of water, baptism by sprinkling "holy water" on a baby's forehead utilized the principle of charging water through prayer before using it as a healing substance.

As a result of such traditions, water still plays an important role in Hawaiian healing rituals and marriage ceremonies. The water is first blessed with prayer in order to give it a charge of energy, or *mana,* and then sprinkled or poured over the person or the ground. At times, it is flicked onto the patient with the tip of a ti leaf while a healing prayer is recited out loud.

P L A N T S

Throughout history, Hawaiians have attributed magical and mysterious powers to plants. For one, plants were considered temporary vehicles for the gods and *aumakuas.* Although these deities' forms could change, they were primarily identified with certain plants, as well as birds and fish. The forms the gods inhabited were called *kinolaus.* The plant *kinolaus* of the four major gods were:

Ku: *'Ohia' lehua,* coconut, breadfruit, and ti
Kane: Sugarcane, certain forms of taro, and popolo
Kanaloa: Banana and *'ala'alapuloa*
Lono: Kukui tree, sweet potato, and a variety of taro

In addition to viewing plants as visible embodiments of the gods, Hawaiians have long used plants for their healing properties. The *kahuna la'au lapa'au* utilized them in their healing work much the same as herbalists do today, except in earlier times the plants were seen more as living beings. Researchers point out that the popolo plant (*Solanum americanum*), one of the embodiments of Kane, was the most important Hawaiian medicinal plant. Before taking its leaves or berries, the *kahuna* would recite a prayer such as the following: "I come to you, Kane Popolo, for a leaf of your body, as medicine for . . ."[19] This plant was used to treat respiratory disorders and skin eruptions as well as to assist in the healing of cuts and wounds.

Noni (*Morinda citrifolia*), which grows wild all over Hawaii today, was also used for wounds and skin eruptions, as well as for boils and sores, whereas kukui (*Aleurites moluccana*) was most commonly used as a laxative, cathartic, or purge. Various varieties of koali (*Ipomea*), or morning glory, were used as a purge alternative to kukui and also as a poultice on broken bones. Kukaepua'a (*Digitaria setigera*), or itchy crabgrass, was used as a painkiller. Not only was its juice applied to relieve pain, but it was regarded as sacred and used in a practice called *la'au kahea,* in which prayers were offered to make the patient's pain disappear.

Awa, a liquid substance made from the root of the awa tree (*Piper methysticum*) is still used as a relaxant in most of the South Pacific. In the past, it was used to alleviate physical ailments such as difficulty in urinating, menstrual irregularities, and congestion, but its most significant function was as an aid to invocation of deities when sipped from coconut husks before important ceremonies.

The bark of hau (*Hibiscus tiliaceus*) and hala flowers were used as laxatives, whereas kalo (*Colocasia esculenta*), or taro, was cooked as a staple of the diet, although raw scrapings were used as medicine. Ohi'a 'ai (*Syzygium malaccense*), or the mountain apple tree, was utilized for sore throats, cuts, and bronchitis, as was uhaloa (*Waltheria indica*), or hialoa, a weed. Even though awapuhi (*Zingiber zerumbet*), or shampoo ginger, was utilized as a remedy for cuts, it is best known today as a shampoo.[20]

Ape leaves (*Alocasia macrorhiza*) were placed under the bed to protect the sleeper from sorcery. Moreover, leaves were used on canoes for protection from storms and high seas and for good luck in fishing. They were also utilized as a tool of divination to tell whether waters were shark infested.

The same respect and focus accompanying prayer, the laying on of hands, and the use of water for healing purposes was also employed in the gathering and administering of healing plants. The usual protocol was to go in search of plants early in the morning when the dew was still on the leaves. Before harvest, prayers were given to Ku if the patient was male and to Hina if the patient was female. For a man the leaves, flowers, or berries were picked with the right hand from the east side of the bush or tree, whereas for a woman they were gathered with the left hand from the west side.

The ti plant (*Cordyline terminalis*), originally known as the ki plant, was among the most useful. Because of their physical properties, the long leaves were used as clothing, food wrappers, thatching for structures, altar decorations, and sometimes food. The most interesting uses of ti leaves, however, were in magic and rituals that drew upon their metaphysical properties. Even today the ti plant is associated with good luck, although its primary function is protection. It was, and still is, planted around houses to safeguard the inhabitants from danger, as well as around the borders of property or near other plants or food crops to protect them. Ti leaves were also placed under the bed or worn around the neck, waist, or ankles of individuals seeking protection.

For direct healing, ti leaves were placed on a person's

body to alleviate simple conditions like headaches, fevers, or stomachaches. To facilitate healing in a more subtle way, they were used by *kahunas* and other individuals to exorcise harmful or negative energies from a person or place. The tip of the leaf was dipped into blessed water and flicked onto the patient or around the area to be blessed, accompanied by prayer.

Undoubtedly one of the most versatile plants used in Hawaiian culture, the ti plant, according to a friend, helped him through some potentially self-destructive times. As he was sitting near the top of a nearby mountain contemplating suicide, he explained, his attention was drawn to a ti plant beside him; he instinctively broke off a branch, put it in his pocket, and brought it home to root on his windowsill. After showing the young plant to me, he acknowledged his gratitude by thanking it for protecting him.

Many other Hawaiian plants have been used to evoke positive feelings, to protect, or to counter evil influences, while some have been utilized for black magic. Plants like pili grass (*Heteropogon contortus*) were used in a ceremony to make one person fall in love with another. The beach morning glory vine known as pohuehue (*Ipomoea pescaprae*) was used for bewitching. An individual who was struck with the vine was believed to encounter serious trouble. This vine was also used to repeatedly whip the surface of the ocean to drown an enemy. In a more benevolent adaptation of this ritual, the vines were recently used to raise the waves for surfing, accompanied by the following chant:

> Arise, arise, ye great surfs from Kahiki
> The powerful curling waves
> Arise with the pohuehue
> Well up, long raging surf.[21]

The leaves and flowers of numerous other Hawaiian plants were used more for their energy properties than for food or medicine. The practice of wearing leis has continued to this day. They are not only given as a symbol of the aloha spirit but also worn for sacred purposes in ceremonies and in dancing the hula.

Interestingly, many of the mysterious powers and extraordinary healing properties Hawaiians attributed to plants have since been validated by scientific research. These findings are discussed in chapter 4.

H O ' O P O N O P O N O

The powerful ancient healing tool known as *ho'oponopono,* a form of communal therapy, is also still practiced today. The word *ho'oponopono* means to make right, to adjust, or to rectify. This approach is first utilized within the family to air grievances and clear the air between family members. Everyone in the family participates, and the session is not complete until all members have expressed their personal issues. The session culminates in forgiveness, reconciliation, and expression of love for all family members.

This practice is also used within groups. With the help of a facilitator, each participant is encouraged to express both positive and negative feedback to other members of the group. Although this process is time-consuming, the intimacy of the participation fosters movement through issues that otherwise seem insurmountable. Because *ho'oponopono* relieves tension and defuses hostility, it allows for the emergence of natural feelings of love and support for one another, assisting true healing.

Having witnessed the dehumanizing effects of traditional problem-solving through lawsuits and court trials, I began encouraging the use of *ho'oponopono* to resolve conflicts. I quickly saw how the honoring of an adversary's opinions and needs can bring to the surface his innate capacity for reason and common sense.

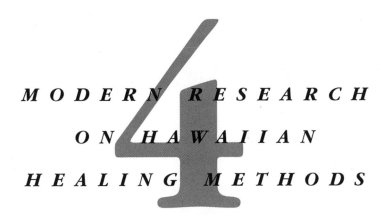

MODERN RESEARCH
ON HAWAIIAN
HEALING METHODS

*S*cientists have investigated many ancient healing practices. Prayer, the laying on of hands, and the use of
water and plants have all been researched and proven
effective.

PRAYER

Considerable research has validated the effects of prayer,
which was used in Hawaiian healing and which I have used
in the creation of flower essences as healing tools. Studies
conducted on both plants and humans have arrived at the
same conclusion: focused prayer results in clinically prov-
able positive changes.

In the 1960s, several studies addressed the positive
effects of prayer on plant seeds. George De La Warr, a civil
engineer, conducted a study showing that the growth rate of

bean seeds was dramatically increased by simply holding the seeds and invoking a blessing.[1] Around the same time, the Loehr Religious Research Foundation reported in its book *The Power of Prayer on Plants* that the growth rate of plants was accelerated by as much as 20 percent when individuals visualized the plants as thriving.[2]

These findings were taken a step further by industrial research scientist Dr. Robert N. Miller in an article entitled "The Positive Effect of Prayer on Plants." He conducted experiments in which he instructed two well-known healers to focus their healing thoughts on rye seedlings six hundred miles away; never before had the effect of thought on plants been monitored at such a distance. Amazingly, he found that the growth rate of the plants was directly affected by the couple's thoughts.[3]

More recent inquiries into the power of prayer on humans have arrived at similar conclusions. More than two hundred studies touch directly or indirectly on the role of prayer and religion in health care, most of them offering evidence that prayer and religion promote well-being.

A 1995 study at Hanover, New Hampshire's Dartmouth-Hitchcock Medical Center found that one of the best predictors of survival among 232 heart surgery patients was the degree to which they believed they received comfort and strength from religious faith. The patients without religious faith had a death rate amounting to more than three times that of those with religious faith.[4]

A survey covering thirty years of research on blood pressure showed that churchgoers had lower blood pressure readings than nonchurchgoers.[5] These findings were confirmed by other studies showing that people who attended church had half the risk of dying from coronary-artery disease compared with those who rarely attended.[6]

A 1996 National Institute on Aging study of 4,000 elderly people living at home in North Carolina found that those who attended religious services were less depressed and physically healthier than those who did not worship. Another study found that nonchurchgoers had a suicide rate four times higher than those who attended church. Moreover, a study of patients recovering from hip fractures revealed that those who regarded God as a source of strength and comfort were able to walk farther upon being discharged and had lower rates of depression than those with little faith.[7]

Finally, in his book *Timeless Healing,* Herbert Benson reported on a group of patients who claimed to have a sense of closeness to God while meditating. After a five-year study, he found that these people had better health and more rapid recoveries than individuals who experienced no sense of closeness to God. Benson concluded that prayer operates along the same biochemical pathways as the relaxation response. In other words, praying affects epinephrine and other corticosteroid messengers, or "stress hormones," leading to lower blood pressure and a more relaxed heart rate and respiration, as well as other physical benefits. He concluded that faith in an invincible and infallible force is wonderfully successful in treating 60 to 90 percent of the most common medical problems.[8]

LAYING ON OF HANDS

The laying on of hands as a healing technique can be traced back to about 1552 B.C. in Egypt. The Greeks later used therapeutic touch in their Asclepian temples for healing the sick. The Bible refers to this method as well; Jesus healed many times with the laying on of hands.

Early Christian churches and the European monarchy also used the laying on of hands for healing purposes. In England, this approach began with Edward the Confessor (1006–1066), and lasted for seven centuries;[9] during that time, many European kings reportedly utilized the power of touch to transfer their healing energy to others. Paracelsus commented on this dynamic when he noted that the vital force was not enclosed inside an individual, but radiated within and around the person like a luminous sphere that could be made to act at a distance.[10]

In 1963, Dr. Bernard Grad published a study entitled "A Telekinetic Effect on Plant Growth," in which he reported that a healer who put his hands on bottles of water later applied to seeds had caused a significant increase in their rate of sprouting.[11] Repeating these tests with various types of psychiatric patients holding bottles of the same solution, he found that negative moods associated with depression, anxiety, or hostility inhibited the growth of the seedlings. In another study he successfully slowed the rate of goiter development in mice by having the lab personnel regularly touch them. In addition, he performed a set of tests on wounded mice showing that they had a significantly faster rate of healing when they were regularly held in healers' hands.[12]

In 1972, Dr. Dolores Krieger followed up on Grad's work by monitoring hemoglobin levels in patients who had undergone a laying on of hands by a recognized healer. She found a significant increase in hemoglobin values among the healer-treated group compared with the control group.[13]

Krieger subsequently repeated the study with a larger group of patients and obtained similar findings. She conducted this research in a practical way by training nurses to use her techniques and studying their results, which showed the same increases in hemoglobin levels. Krieger concluded that therapeutic touch is a natural human potential that can be demonstrated by individuals who have a healthy body and a strong intent to help or heal ill people.[14]

It is clear from this research that the laying on of hands brings about significant healing through the transfer from healer to patient of some type of life force. Although this technique was labeled "witchcraft" in American colonial times, Hawaiians had successfully used it for centuries before it became associated with the devil. The exact name for the force at work is not as important as the fact that researchers have confirmed that healing takes place on a metaphysical or vibrational level through human touch. What a great service every one of us would perform if we remembered to silently recite a simple prayer while embracing others or shaking hands with them.

W A T E R

French researchers have established that water brought in contact with a healer's touch and focused thoughts becomes infused with a charge of some form of measurable energy. They found water to be a strange medium, for it was normally unradiant but was capable of being vitalized by association with minerals, plants, human beings, or the sun. Some of the energized water samples were radiating at the extremely high level of 156,000 angstroms; when the water was retested eight years later, it still registered 78,000 angstroms.[15]

Other researchers have discovered that water can be charged with energy that registers as a magnetic force. They found that the force in bottled water charged by healers could be transmitted to sick patients through the use of metallic rods held in the patients' hands.[16]

Such research indicates that human health may be significantly improved if individuals began taking time to consciously charge the water they drink. By combining the power of prayer and the laying on of hands, this can be accomplished by *anyone* who is willing to effectively pray while holding a bottle or glass of water. Drinking charged water would enable people to benefit from moments of spiritual focus any time that clarity became difficult to access.

Based on the characteristics documented by present-day research, water can be used as a medium to hold the energy patterns of flower and gem essences. While making such essences, the preparer uses focused prayer and the charge of their hands to energize the water containing the flower or gem. In fact, without the use of such charged water and the sun, the energetic healing properties of flowers and gems could not be put into a consumable form. The added use of focused prayer results in especially potent essences.

P L A N T S

Numerous researchers have shown that plants respond to thought and other stimuli, and have a life force. In the 1960s Cleve Backster, the top lie-detector examiner in America, used a modified lie detector on plants and, to his amazement, found that they can think. Plants reacted in advance of Backster's intention to pour hot water on them and before he lit a match with which he planned to burn them. He also observed that plants react not only to their own impending danger but to the danger faced by animals, insects, or humans in the room. This unusual intelligence of plants was even recorded when the examiner performed stimulating tests *fifteen miles away* from their location.[17]

A Russian researcher, V. N. Pushkin, conducted similar

tests, postulating that the reason for the connection between the plant and the person applying stimulation was that a unique link exists between plant cells and the human nervous system. Pushkin concluded that the "language" of plant cells and human nerve cells may be related, and that these entirely different cells seem capable of understanding each other.[18]

Many other researchers have obtained positive responses while testing plants' reactions to stimuli such as music, projections of love, and magnetism. The famous scientist and engineer Marcel Vogel, who conducted extensive testing of the capabilities of plants, concluded: "Man can and does communicate with plant life. Plants are living objects, sensitive, rooted in space. They may be blind, deaf and dumb in the human sense, but there is no doubt in my mind that they are extremely sensitive instruments for measuring man's emotions. They radiate energy forces that are beneficial to man. One can feel these forces! They feed into one's own force field, which in turn feeds back into the energy of the plants."[19]

In conclusion, a body of research on the power of prayer, the laying on of hands, the charging of water, and the intelligence of plants has collectively confirmed the presence of a life force, or *mana,* which Hawaiians have long understood to be the force behind all living things. By embracing the best of traditional Hawaiian healing practices, knowing that they have been confirmed by modern science, we can recapture some of the magic that sustained these people.

THE 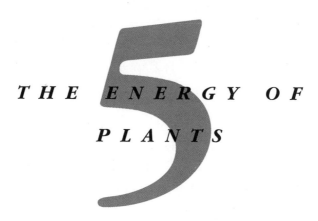ENERGY OF PLANTS

*T*he concept that everything consists of energy was made visible when the technology of Kirlian photography, or electrophotography, was developed in 1940. Electrophotography records the electrical field, or corona discharge, of living things. Through the use of Kirlian photography on plants, some dramatic effects have been recorded that verify the existence of energy fields.

Numerous researchers, for example, have reported a phenomenon known as the "phantom leaf effect," or "ghost effect." After cutting off the outer third of a leaf and then taking a Kirlian photograph of the remaining leaf, the resulting image shows the outer portion still attached.[1] This phantom leaf effect indicates the existence of an energy or spirit form around plants. Such energy forms have also been shown around humans; these are generally ignored, however, despite the fact that they work silently to keep us alive, as well as maintain templates of our energy, even after the removal of a limb.

In 1982 I. Dumitrescu, a Rumanian scientist, made an even more striking observation after cutting a circular hole in a leaf and taking a Kirlian photograph of the leaf. This image showed the original leaf with a tiny leaf appearing within the cut-out hole and a smaller hole appearing within it.[2] Such findings indicate that there is more to the energy fields of living things than the energy bodies surrounding them. They establish that plants, and by extension all living things, are really holograms as well, with one part capable of producing the whole.

Recently, various authors and channels have added to our understanding of energy in plants and humans. Machaelle Small Wright, who has channeled much valuable information on the subject in her book *Dancing in the Shadows of the Moon,* quotes a nature force as saying the following: "All energy contains order, organization, and life vitality; therefore, all energy is form. From our perspective, form and energy create one unit of reality and are differentiated from one another solely by the individual's ability to perceive them with his or her sensory system."[3]

Moreover, Michael J. Roads, an Australian author and channel, quotes the same nature force as saying: "The plants around you are filled with energy; all life is energy. This is yours if only you can be aware that you are not separate; you are part of a Whole. Be open, be loving. Become All in One, the One in All."[4]

In Hawaii the idea that plants have energy is easy to accept, since the concept of *mana,* or life force, is associated with them. In my own interaction with plants, I have observed and felt their energy, and in some cases, their thoughts, or the thoughts of an energy connected with them. Because these plant spirits have supported and nurtured me, I trust them to make the right decisions when I need information about whether a plant or tree requires more water or a particular type or quantity of fertilizer. I also trust the energy of my guides who, working with the plant devas, tell me which plants will be most effective in healing me or those I help as a flower essence practitioner.

F L O W E R S

For centuries, flowers have been eulogized in songs, drama, and poetry. Often, they have been associated with perfection and divinity, as in the following poem by Alfred Lord Tennyson:

> Flower in the crannied wall,
> I pluck you out of the crannies,
> I hold you here, rooted and all, in my hand,
> Little flower—but if I could understand
> What you are, root and all, and all in all,
> I should know what God and man is.[5]

This poem captures the sense of awe and wonder we feel when we look closely at a flower, at its intricate detail and vibrant colors. Since flowers represent the crowning stage of growth and vitality for many plants, the sudden appearance of a flower among stems might be compared to the wondrous metamorphosis of a caterpillar into a butterfly.

We have all experienced the energy and presence of flowers. They turn themselves to the sun, radiating their energy out like tiny antennas. Many of them even display their sex organs in a way that would no doubt be considered exhibitionist if they were humans. Their state of existence—without concern, and beyond moral and religious precepts—is one of the best-known metaphors for an ideal human existence addressed in the Bible. Jesus instructed: "Consider the lilies, how they grow; they neither toil nor spin; yet I tell you, even Solomon, in all his glory was not arrayed like one of these."[6]

Hawaii has been blessed with a location and climate that support the world's most diverse collection of flowers. Their scent and beauty, an intricate part of the Hawaiian atmosphere, infuse and color the landscape that attracts so many people every year. Because their scent has a calming, healing, or stimulating effect, it is not surprising that many Hawaiian hulas are about flowers and their fragrances. Hawaiian hula is living theater, danced as an accompaniment to poetic chants, or *mele,* as well as a religious rite dedicated to Laka, goddess of the hula.

The modern *kahuna* and teacher Serge Kahili King, in his book *Kahuna Healing,* describes an interesting historical use of the scent of flowers for healing. *Kahunas* reportedly had their patients inhale the fragrances directly. The belief was that the essence of the material inhaled would go directly to the bloodstream via the lungs and act more quickly than if the flower were swallowed.[7]

Russians have used the scent of flowers in a similar way. In sanitariums near the Black Sea, aging Russians afflicted with either physical or mental problems are treated not with drugs, but with flowers. Every day, the patients are taken to greenhouses, where they are left to sit and smell specific blooms.[8]

There is little doubt that flowers are emotionally uplifting. Even in hospital rooms their fragrance and beauty may stimulate some tangible healing action. Perhaps if this healing effect were recognized and flowers were prescribed by doctors, the purchase of them would be a health-care expense deductible from our income taxes!

H O M E O P A T H Y

Homeopathy was introduced in the treatise *The Organon of Medicine* by German physician Samuel Hahnemann (1755–1843), who discovered that giving a patient a small dose of a substance capable of producing symptoms of an illness similar to the one the patient was attempting to cure resulted in a return to health. He then reasoned that an individual's personality played a role in illness, and that a tiny amount of a substance corresponding to that personality type would alleviate the body's disease. This philosophy led to the creation of a school of medicine based on the use of small amounts of specific plants or other natural substances to heal particular conditions.

The amounts of plants and other substances used in homeopathic medicines are so minute that they no longer contain any of their former chemical properties. Only their subtle energy qualities, absorbed into water, are placed on the tablet. Despite this fact—or perhaps because of it—healing does occur; indeed, many people around the world now use this form of medicine exclusively. Hahnemann's discovery of homeopathy expanded medical thought in his times, and in ours has inspired individuals to look farther outside of mainstream medicine for exciting new methods of healing.

B A C H   F L O W E R   R E M E D I E S

Although many cultures have utilized the fragrances of flowers either ceremonially or to promote health, not until Dr. Edward Bach (1886–1936) of England began experimenting with their healing properties did the modern world start to focus on the use of flowers for healing. All his life, Bach had a deep love of nature. Nevertheless, for sixteen years he worked in London and spent little time in the countryside, because he thought it would be difficult to readjust to the conditions of city life following an immersion in the energies of nature.

After practicing allopathic medicine for four years, Bach embarked on an eleven-year practice of homeopathic medicine, during which time he isolated a type of bacteria from the gastrointestinal tracts of people suffering from chronic illnesses such as arthritis. He speculated that inoculation with vaccines made from these intestinal bacteria would have the desired effect of cleansing the system of bacterial poisons causing the chronic illnesses. The diluted vaccines produced significant improvements in the patients' arthritis symptoms, a result similar to those achieved by other homeopathic doctors.

In addition, Bach hypothesized that people could be divided into different personality types—an observation that opened the door to radical new discoveries. He noted that individuals belonging to the same personality group would not necessarily come down with the same diseases but would, when exposed to a disease-causing agent, react to illness in a similar manner. In addition to personality factors, he observed that different emotions served as predisposing factors to particular illnesses. Once these emotional conditions were remedied, people's vitality seemed to increase *and* their physical diseases were cured.

An even more significant revelation was Bach's discovery of *the healing agent* used to correct the illnesses diagnosed by personality type. The great revelation was not simply that flowers had a healing function when given in small doses, or the selection of thirty-eight specific English flowers to make into remedies. It was that the *dew* on the flower contained properties of the plant, and that the sun's heat, acting through the fluid, would draw out these properties until each drop was magnetized with power.

Bach summarized his philosophy on healing in the following statement: "From time immemorial it has been known that Providential Means have placed in nature the prevention and cure of disease, by means of divinely enriched herbs and plants and trees. They have been given the power to heal all types of illness and suffering. In treating cases with these remedies no notice is taken of the nature of the disease. The individual is treated, and as he becomes well the disease goes, having been cast off by the increase in health. The mind, being the most delicate and sensitive part of the body, shows the onset and course of the disease much more definitely than the body, so that the outlook of mind is chosen as the guide as to which remedy or remedies is necessary."[9]

Bach's initial production of flower remedies entailed harvesting the dew from individual flowers. Because this was a time-consuming task capable of producing only minuscule amounts of essence, he later changed the procedure to picking a few blossoms, placing them in a glass bowl filled with clear stream water, and letting them sit in a sunny field for several hours.

Reportedly, Bach believed that no essences were necessary beyond the thirty-eight he had created; however, some people have speculated that his death at age fifty could have been delayed if he had broadened his selection of flowers, as has since been done by others. Today, there are many producers of flower essences throughout the world. Indeed, the enormous variety of flowers on our planet allows for an almost infinite number of potential flower essences.

U S E S   O F   F L O W E R   E S S E N C E S

Flowers have been used as healing agents in the form of teas, tinctures, homeopathic medicines, and flower essences. The earliest recorded attempt to determine specific uses of flowers and flower essences was conducted by Paracelsus in the 1500s and was called the "doctrine of signatures." It stated that the shape, size, and color of a plant should all be considered in determining the physical organ, body part, or condition the plant can be used to treat.[10] Obvious examples of this correspondence between physical aspects of plants and their healing functions are banana and banana poka; the shape of the fruits suggest their healing connection with the penis. Another example is beach heliotrope, whose fruit resembles the lung and is associated with improved breathing after excessive crying. The tree itself grows in the spray of the ocean which, like tears, is salty to the taste.

More recently, the focus has shifted from the physical properties of flowers and fruits to their energy qualities, as refined by well-recognized flower essence creators and practitioners. Most currently recommended medicinal uses are based on a mixture of information from the doctrine of signatures, intuitive or channeled revelations, and case histories containing documented outcomes from taking various flower essences.

This shift in focus has given rise to four methods now used to discover the conditions a given flower essence will treat. The first of these methods is to concentrate on the energy of the plant and write down or tape-record the information that comes to mind. Interestingly, applications received in this way are often remarkably similar to those published in most medicinal repertories. Further information can be obtained by observing and recording your own reactions after taking the essence.

A second method for acquiring treatment information is a system of muscle testing, such as kinesiology, used in connection with statements made while concentrating on the energy of the plant. Kinesiology is a means of testing the body's response to pressure exerted on the arm, the fingers, or the leg. By pressing down on a person's arm, you can measure the truth of her statements. If the information stated about the plant is true, the arm will remain rigid, resisting this downward push; if it is false, the energy current that naturally flows through the electrical grid of the body will be broken, and the arm will fall. This test can also be conducted on the fingers by forming a loop with the thumb and pinkie, then exerting force with your other thumb and forefinger in an attempt to break the loop. When correct information is stated, the fingers will remain strong, and vice versa. For further information, research the many books available on kinesiology or locate a practitioner who can help you better understand this method.

A third means of getting information from a plant about its possible medicinal benefits is through dowsing, or the use of a pendulum. This instrument, like muscle testing, elicits "yes" or "no" responses. The response to each question will come through the movement of the pendulum as it swings either left to right, backward and forward, or in a circular motion. In advance, each of these movements must be ascribed a meaning by the person using the pendulum and must be clearly understood by the subconscious mind. I have always considered left to right (like the shaking of the head from side to side) to indicate a "no" response and a backward and forward motion (like a positive nodding of the head) to indicate a "yes." According to some dowsing systems, a clockwise circular motion indicates "yes," and a counterclockwise motion "no."

Dowsing is an ancient art used for finding water, minerals, and objects that have a natural magnetic, electromagnetic, or other form of energy. In addition to the pendulum, dowsers' tools have included a Y-shaped stick and an L-rod, all of which served to link the human senses with the natural world. Although *kahunas* have possessed varying degrees of this heightened sensory capacity, it is unclear whether or not they used dowsing devices.

A final method for obtaining knowledge of a plant or flower's specific effects is to connect with the spiritual energy or being inhabiting the plant. The ancient Hawaiians directed their prayers and thoughts to the god, goddess, or *aumakua* associated with a plant. In other words, when addressing a plant, they were really sending their prayer to the deity it embodied. Most modern authors who write about flower essences describe the deity connected with each plant as a "deva," or nature spirit. These beings have been eulogized by poets such as Shakespeare, and appear in mythology throughout the world, although each culture has its own understanding of them. Devas are said to inhabit all members of a plant species, and hence it is possible to communicate with the deva of a species through an individual plant. Other than offering the customary respect, no formalities are required when asking questions and receiving answers.

The author Gurudas has published a wonderful book on flower essences, in which he describes the nature of devas as follows: "As ye draw in oxygen from the atmosphere, so in turn the devas in their existence are electromagnetic beings in same. Even as ye draw nutritional elements from the energy of the sun for thy physical bodies, so in turn the nutritional elements relevant in the perspective of the devic beings concern the aspects of their needs from the essences.

The actual essence, of course, is the electromagnetic pattern of the plant form. Even as there are nutritional elements found in various plant forms that ye partake of for the physical body, so in turn are there various patterns of biomagnetic energies discharged by flowers and various plant forms. And the vitality of the life force increases about the area of the bloom. The biomagnetic properties of the plants aid in maintaining the electromagnetic form of the devas."[11]

In communicating with devas, various problems can arise. Although scientists have shown that plants and people possess the ability to communicate with each other, communication between plants and people is often confused by different understandings of what words really mean, as is often the case between humans. In addition to the problem of different meanings, it is necessary to clarify the energy with whom you are communicating and pose questions accordingly. When using kinesiology or a pendulum to inquire about a health condition you may have and which flower essence would remedy it, there are two distinct possibilities: you may be questioning your own subconscious or you may be communicating with the flower or plant deva. In the latter case, you will want to direct your questions or thoughts to the deva itself.

Another problem that sometimes arises is the unwillingness to say what is really meant. It does no good to have a great connection with a deva but not be able to speak the truth and thus obtain reliable answers. Unfortunately, our society has developed a tolerance, often a preference, for veiling the true meaning of words. It may be, as Bach speculated, that because our emotional natures are so sensitive, we are in constant fear of being told "no" when we need to hear "yes."[12] If so, it is fear that prevents us from "speaking our truth."

In my experience, devas have no reason to lie, and their desire to communicate is frustrated only by the fact that humans persist in perceiving lying as useful. Therefore, to increase the likelihood of getting accurate responses when communicating with a deva, it is necessary to ask clear, unambiguous questions that reflect the truth.

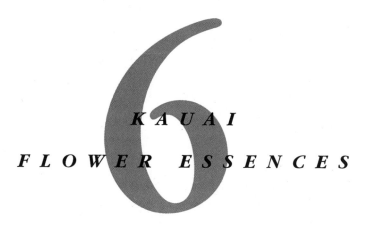

6

KAUAI
FLOWER ESSENCES

ince the magical energy of Kauai, the "Garden Island," supports some of the most vibrant plants and flowers in the world, my awakening to the healing potential of flowers could not have occurred in a more perfect place. My longtime friend Roger Denisewicz joined me in exploring Kauai's coastal areas, tropical rain forests, inland marshes, and mountain crevices searching for special flowers. We were soon communicating directly with the plants in an effort to determine which flowers had special healing properties.

After several expeditions, we developed a method similar to Bach's for preparing flower essences from the natural blossoms we found. We exposed flowers to the sun for a longer period of time, however, and invoked the participation of numerous spirit beings in the process. The deva, or spirit, of each plant told me how many blooms were needed to make the essence; then we picked the flowers without touching them and dropped them onto water. Rather than using water from a stream, as Bach did, we used distilled water and water from Kauai's streams that had been filtered through three membranes.

The next step was the most important. While holding my hands outside of the bowl of water and directing my focus into the water, I asked for the blessing and assistance of my guides. I then engaged the deva of the plant whose flowers were in the water, and explained what I was doing and why.

Finally, addressing all these higher powers collectively, I asked them to support the deva of the particular flower in transferring its unique life force and energy signature to the water, explaining that the energy of the flowers was not being destroyed but was being made immortal in the form of the water. "Begin transferring your energy now!" I would say, and in that instant I would often feel surges of tingling energy or a sudden jolt as the transformation began. Thus, the flower essences I began midwifing consisted of the flowers' energy signature stabilized in water and charged with *mana* through focused prayer and the laying on of hands.

The transformation itself was fascinating. It was as if the devas were poised, waiting for me to request their help in metamorphosing the flowers into a form that would benefit the most people. Alick McIness, a Scotsman who produced flower essences, said that in this moment of energy transfer into water, he could actually see the water change and observe other members of the same flower species for miles around brighten up and grow more vigorously.[1]

As time passed, Roger and I decided to form a company, at which point the concept of going beyond limited thinking became increasingly important. The reason was that the difficulties we sometimes faced, we realized, were usually caused by limited thinking, like forgetting to ask for the help and wisdom of our guides and the devas. To affirm our commitment to refrain from limited thinking, we named our company Starmen Unlimited.

The concept of going beyond limited thinking also inspired the creation of several programs to release "stuck" energy. In particular human patterns, energy seemed to be getting stuck, or limited, and we found that these frozen patterns could be released and disappear when certain essences were taken over a period of time. This releasing capacity was especially pronounced with the use of Kauai flower essences that work on fear-based sexual patterns.

Roger and I knew from the start that our energy subtly influenced the vibration of each essence, and we made every effort to minimize such influence. We also knew, however, that any vibrational medicine—including homeopathic and even acupuncture—was subject to this type of infringement, and that in the manufacture of some Vedic medicines, workers were instructed to chant mantras to make sure their energy influence on the medicines would be positive. We, too, carefully monitored our energy while working with the essences, so that the minuscule vibrational influences we were imparting would be positive.

As Starmen Unlimited grew, we became obsessed with protecting the integrity of each essence during production and bottling. The increasing number of people who were enjoying our essences, we knew, wanted to receive the five-million-year-old energies of the Garden Island of Kauai, along with the devic energies of the plants themselves—as free of outside vibrations as possible.

Currently, eighty-two flower essences are available to the public through Starmen Unlimited. Others have been produced, are being tested, and will be added to our list when we are certain that they offer additional possibilities for healing. Many of the flower essences we produce are not available anywhere else. Eric Pelham, a highly telepathic Englishman, has provided us with detailed descriptions of the properties of the essences, as well as devic analyses of them, many of which appear on pages 117–141.

Starmen Unlimited's flower essences are available in stock bottles, each of which contains one dilution from the original mother tincture—generally considered the most effective dose, and the one available from most other flower essence practitioners. Although the stock can be further diluted, if desired, I have been guided by the energies working with me to provide flower essences at an enhanced stock-bottle strength by adding ten drops of the mother tincture rather than the usual seven.

The flower essences can be used in a variety of ways. They may be taken in the form of drops, directly into the mouth, on the skin, or in a bath or beverage. Many Hawaiian *lomi lomi* (practitioners of an ancient temple massage technique) and other massage practitioners, use our flower essences in their massage oils by adding seven to ten drops to a one-ounce vial of oil and shaking the mixture to reactivate it in its new form. Numerous other people add ten drops to a water bottle in the morning and drink the diluted dosage throughout the course of the day.

The essences are mixed in a solution of 60 percent triple-filtered Kauai water and 40 percent brandy, which preserves the essence indefinitely and stabilizes its energy. For individuals who object to the small amount of alcohol present in the drops, we recommend either diluting the essence in a glass of water or putting it in a cup of tea, which will evaporate the alcohol.

The flower essences affect people to varying degrees. Those who are highly sensitive feel energetic changes within seconds of taking an essence. Others are gradually able to make and hold changes on the physical, emotional, mental, and spiritual levels. All these shifts are facilitated by the capacity of the energy medicines to subtly work on the etheric, astral, mental, and causal energy planes. Because the flower essences are self-adjusting, they have no negative effect if too much is taken.

The highest levels of effectiveness are obtained when the flower essences are taken in an atmosphere of quiet relaxation and a mood of focused prayer, as discussed in chapter 3. The devas are available to assist you, and it is strongly recommended that you extend gratitude to them while taking an essence. It is also advisable to hold clearly in your mind the condition for which you seek help or the emotional, mental, or spiritual area that needs fine-tuning. When healing with flower essences, that is precisely what you will be doing—fine-tuning your energetic system.

Selecting a flower essence to suit your needs can be accomplished through intuition, through kinesiology, by using a pendulum, or by asking the devas of select flowers. Most flower essence practitioners are adept at this art and can also help you achieve maximum benefit from the chosen essence. I take essences daily, selecting the ones I need by asking my guides for assistance in assessing my condition and deciding on the appropriate remedy. As they link with the energy of one essence after another, I identify the most useful one via kinesiology. This method is enormously effective, but to use it you will need several different essences on hand so that your guides will have a sufficient number of healing energies from which to choose.

Another way of assessing the flower essence most directly associated with the issue at hand is by studying the properties of the essences. Because the properties attributed to flower essences can vary from source to source, and a complete listing would therefore be unwieldy, we have reduced the property descriptions of Starmen Unlimited's essences to those with which many different sources generally agree.

The following are the Kauai Flower Essences produced by Starmen Unlimited, along with their properties.

S T A R M E N   U N L I M I T E D ' S FLOWER ESSENCES

African Tulip (*Spathodea camanulata*)—Liberates from the effects of past-life associations with dark forces. Prolonged use required.

Aloe Vera (*Aloe vera;* Hawaiian: *Panini-awa'awa*)—Revitalizes the etheric body and nervous system. Closes "holes" in the aura caused by burnout and psychotropic drugs.

Angel's Trumpet (*Datura candida;* Hawaiian: *Nana-honu*)—For soul-level guidance from angels. Clarifies intellectual functions and enhances visions. Facilitates spiritual surrender.

Avocado (*Persea americana*)—Overcomes the fear of being touched and opens sensitivity to touch.

Banana (*Musa saprentum;* Hawaiian: *Mai'a*)—Balances the sexual energy of men, reducing excessive sexual energy or increasing sex drive if it is too weak.

Banana Poka (*Passiflora mollissina*) Balances and rejuvenates the male sex drive. Improves the physical action of the penis in sexual intercourse.

Basil (*Ocimum basilicum*)—Good for bickering couples. Facilitates negotiation and helps clarify emotional issues. Relieves polarized sexual issues.

Beach Heliotrope (*Heliotropium curasavicum*)—For children's excessive crying and grief. Restores well-being, calmness, and strength.

Bird of Paradise (*Strelitzia reginae*)—Supports individual freedom and sense of interconnectedness among people.

Bougainvillea (*Bougainvillea spectabilis*, var. *lateritia*)— Rekindles inspiration and restores the vision of a higher spiritual path.

Canavalia (*Canavalia maritima*)—Restores inner certainty and bridges the connection with the higher self.

Canna Lily (*Canna indica*)—Restores the love and compassion compromised in the present or a past lifetime. Deeply healing.

Castor Bean (*Ricinus communis L.;* Hawaiian: *La'au'-aila*)—Calms and strengthens women with deep fears and anxieties.

Christmas Berry (*Schinus terebinthfolius*)—Aids recuperation from alcohol hangovers and aftereffects of the amphetamine MDNA, or ecstasy. Acts as a detox from alcohol or ecstasy dependency.

Coconut (*Cocos nucifera;* Hawaiian: *Niu*)—Corrects psychological imbalances and diminishes confusion about sexuality.

Comfrey (*Symphytum peregrinum*)—Helps release tension in the nervous system and subconscious. Enhances telepathic and mental abilities.

Corn (*Zea mays*)—Assists urban dwellers in maintaining spiritual contact with the earth. Bridges experience, understanding, and action.

Cosmos (*Cosmos bipinnatus*)—Calms and aids the integration of clear thoughts and ideas into speech.

Cotton (*Gossypium barbadense*)—Invigorates the hair all over the body. Releases fear.

Dahlia (*Dahlia pinnata Cav.*)—Activates emotional resiliency and stamina during extreme emotional stress, leading to optimism.

Dandelion (*Taaraxacum officiale*)—Relieves tensions in the body.

False Lilac (*Budleia asiatica*)—Cleanses the will and dissolves the energy blocking personal power.

Gardenia (*Ervatamia divaricata*)—Creates feelings of compassion and peace. Aids attunement after a recent shift in consciousness.

Geranium (*Geranium cuneatum,* var. *tridens*)—Helps in understanding, balancing, and healing past relationships.

Glory Bush (*Tibouchina urvilleana*)—Diminishes fears associated with past-life cruelty in group situations. Aids relaxation.

Golden Amaranth (*Amaranthus spinosus*)—Boosts the immune system to repel viral infections in the solar plexus and intestinal areas.

Gomphrena-bozo (*Gomphrena globosa*)—Diplomat's essence. An adaptation and attunement for those traveling to a foreign country or otherwise experiencing another culture.

Haole Koa (*Leucaena latisiliqua*)—Dissolves negative conditioned attitudes about sex and revitalizes the flow of sexual energy.

Hau (*Hibiscus tiliaceus*)—Eases tension in stressful situations.

Heliconia (*Heliconia mairiae*)—Helps in assimilating ideas and making changes. Enhances brain function.

Hibiscus (*Hibiscus rosa-sinensis*)—Frees blocked sexual energy in women.

Hila Hila (*Mimosa pudica L.*)—Restores wholeness to the mind, overcoming toxicity from other people's derogatory thoughts.

Impatiens (*Imatiens gladulifera*)—Restores patience and tolerance.

Kou (*Cordia subcordata*)—Enhances clairvoyant abilities and clarity of perception.

Kukui (*Aleurites moluccana*)—Enhances calmness and the understanding of emotions.

Lantana (*Lantana camara L.*)—Harmonizes conflicting emotions, promoting the release of sadness and pain through tears.

Lehua (*Metrosideros collina*)—Increases female sexual energy and self-esteem, restoring balance and enjoyment.

Lemon (*Citrus limon*)—Invigorates the mental body and meridians.

Lima Bean (*Phaseolus limensis*)—Grounds.

Lime (*Citrus aurantiiflia*)—Attunes the consciousness to the higher self. Opens the sixth and seventh chakras.

Lotus (*Nelumbo nuciera*)—Master healer. Balances all the chakras. Accelerates the process of enlightenment. Balances the spiritual ego.

Macadamia (*Macadamia ternifolia*)—Alleviates mild tensions between couples and enhances friendship.

Mango (*Mangifera indica*)—Universal tonic. Stimulates telepathy. Energizes.

Marigold (*Tagetes minuta L.*)—Enhances joy of life in a physical body.

Mock Orange (*Murraya exotica*)—Energizes and resensitizes the nervous system after overwork, stress, or trauma. Functions as a general pick-me-up.

Morning Glory (*Ipomea purpurea*)—Helps overcome nicotine and opiate addictions. Revitalizes the nervous system. Remedies hangover.

Naio (*Myoporum sandwicense*)—Aids weight loss by alleviating addiction to the pleasure of eating.

Nasturtium (*Tropaeolum majus*)—Eases nervousness and modifies obsessive behavior. Increases vitality.

Naupaka kahakai (*Scaevola taccada*) and **Naupaka kuahiwi** (*Scaevola gaudichaudiana*)—Heals mental negativity of people attached to earthly power.

Nicotiana (*Nicotiana alata*)—Activates deadened feelings. Facilitates connection to Mother Earth for emotional wholeness.

Noni (*Morinda citrifolia*)—Strengthens health and emotions for pregnancy and childbirth.

Oleander (*Nerium oleander*)—Alleviates deeply buried emotional problems that cause withdrawal.

Orange (*Citrus sinensia*)—Restores clarity and calmness in highly charged emotional states. Releases deep subconscious tensions.

Orchid (*Epidendrum X obrrenianum*)—Clarifies dreams. Balances emotions in times of extreme stress.

Paka Lana (*Telosma cordata*)—Works on the highest spiritual vibrations of the self to restore the clear direction of inner light.

Papaya (*Carica papaya*)—Provides greater insight into the repressed male and female aspects of a person. Enhances clarity in couple relationships.

Papyrus (*Cyperus papyrus;* Hawaiian: *Kaluha* or *Papulo*)—Improves communication and negotiation skills. Enhances flexibility in pursuit of higher goals.

Passion Flower (*Passiflora*)—Aids in perception of Christ consciousness. Deepens spiritual confidence.

Pineapple (*Ananas comosus*)—Opens and amplifies the chakras. Cleanses the meridians.

Plumeria (*Plumeria acuminata P. acutiflia;* Hawaiian: *Pua melia*)—Brings awareness of family roots. Restores spiritual integrity for Native peoples.

Poha (*Physalis peruviana;* Hawaiian: *Pa'ina*)—Enhances learning abilities of children who have had negative relationships with family or friends.

Poinsettia (*Euphoria pulcherrima*)—Opens the first chakra and balances the lower-chakra energy to enhance upward motion.

Pua Kenikeni (*Fagraea berteriana*)—Eases craving for physical pleasure and marijuana.

Red Ginger (*Alinia purpurata;* Hawaiian: *'Awapuhi 'ula'ula*)—Moves the male-female union into its highest aspects.

Rosemary (*Rosmarinus L.*)—Balances the emotional body. Enhances creativity. Promotes inner peace.

Shower Tree (*Cassia javanica L.*)—Aids peacemaking between people of different cultures and languages by alleviating fear and suspicion.

Snapdragon (*Antirrhinum majus*)—Aids speech problems. For jaw, mouth, and TMJ disorders due to prolonged verbal aggression and hostility.

Spider Lily (*Hymenocallis littoralis*)—Dissolves negative attitudes about women in men.

Spilanthes (*Spilanthes acmella*)—Clarifies issues associated with a man's sexual compatibility with a particular woman and allows the higher will and destiny to take control.

Strawberry (*Fragaria chiloensis*)—Stimulates visions and eases mental rigidity.

Sugarcane (*Saccharum*)—Counteracts sudden mood swings, lethargy, and depression.

Sunflower (*Helianthus annuus L.*)—Tempers and spiritualizes the male ego for a balanced sense of individuality.

Sweet Potato (*Ipomomea batatas;* Hawaiian: *Uala*)—Assists the healing of young children who have experienced trauma or an accident.

Thyme (*Thymus vulgaris*)—Amplifies the effects of other flower essences. Speeds up time flow.

Ti (*Cordyline terminalis*)—Lifts spells or curses. Eliminates astral possession.

Tomato (*Lycopersicon*)—Opens the base chakra. Assists the body in eliminating the cause of infection or disease.

Vervain (*Verbenaceae*)—Alleviates nervous stress or tension. Induces sleep. Promotes balance.

Water Hyacinth (*Eichhornia crassipes*)—Cleanses the emotions, lifting depression, fear, and heaviness. Good for the winter blues or lack of sun.

Water Lily (*Nymphaea*)—Enriches the exciting and erotic aspects of lovemaking.

Wood Rose (*Ipomoea tuberosa*)—Alleviates nervous tension and stress due to overwork and fear.

Yellow Ginger (*Heychium flavum;* Hawaiian: *Awapuhi-melemele*)—Aligns the physical and astral bodies, releasing subconscious agitating issues. Induces sleep.

Zinnia (*Zinnia elegans;* Hawaiian: *Pua pihi*)—Restores playfulness and contact with the inner child. Facilitates a positive outlook on life.

7

G E M   E S S E N C E S

*G*em essences are tinctures of liquid energy that carry the same vibrational properties as the gem they are made from. They can have a powerful effect on the chakras, meridians, and subtle energy fields. Because certain gemstones have a special harmonic resonance with particular points in the body, an essence made from such a gem will resonate with those points. Water is a proven storage medium for vibrational energy, and sunlight has the ability to help draw properties out of a substance into water. Gem essences are made with the aid of sun and water, using a method similar to the one for making flower essences.

Gurudas, with the assistance of psychic Kevin Ryerson, has written the most respected work on gem essences, *Gem Elixirs and Vibrational Healing,* in which they discuss the difference between gem essences and flower essences: "Gemstones function between flower essences and homeopathic remedies. When a physical gemstone is ingested after being crushed, it is closer to homeopathy and notably influences the physical body with medicinal, nutritional, and antibiotic properties. When a gem is prepared into an elixir, however, using the sun in a method similar to preparing flower essences, that remedy functions slightly closer to flower essences and is more ethereal in its properties."[1]

The gem essences Starmen Unlimited has created address conditions grounded primarily in the physical body. Because these essences, like the flower essences, affect the physical body as well as the etheric bodies, they provide an additional vibratory tool for healing work.

In creating our gem essences, Roger and I were fortunate to have the assistance of Jim Saylor, a fine local jeweler, and Katrina Raphaell, a leading authority on crystals and the author of several books on the subject. We first selected gemstones that were natural (uncut and unpolished) and that appeared to have a high degree of purity. Before making the essences, we cleansed the gems in the ocean, left them overnight under the moon and stars, and made sure they absorbed the first rays of the morning sun.

In producing the gem essences, we adhered to the same form of prayer and ritual used in making flower essences, but with one difference: the nature spirits we communicated with were addressed as guardians of the gems rather than as devas. We placed each gem in a bowl of water for approximately four hours, then we asked spiritual allies to assist us and held our hands around the bowl while focusing on the gem within. My physical reactions, as I asked the guardians of the gems to transmute their energy into the water, were often more powerful than those I experienced with the flowers, and more of the gems' healing properties were revealed.

The process of determining the function of various gem

essences is similar to that for flower essences. We have delin-
eated the uses of each gem essence by combining the best
of the gem-healing definitions from Katrina Raphaell and
Gurudas with our own.

Dosages for the gem essences are the same as for the
flower essences, except that the gem essences are not self-
correcting, so it is important not to take excessive doses of
the wrong one. Three to four drops in the mouth three times
a day is plenty.

The following are the forty-two gem essences offered by
Starmen Unlimited, along with their healing qualities.

S T A R M E N   U N L I M I T E D ' S
G E M   E S S E N C E S

Amazonite—Enhances most vibrational remedies. Magnifies
the energy stored in the heart and solar plexus and aligns
the etheric and mental bodies.

Amethyst—Enhances mental clarity and strengthens the
willpower to break undesirable habits. Calms the mind
for meditation. Induces sleep. Aids left-brain imbalances.
Eases spasms.

Azurite—Stimulates psychic abilities and higher inspiration.
Promotes clearer meditations and increased mental control.

Black Tourmaline—Provides psychic protection and grounding for spiritual awareness in the third dimension. Aids city
life functioning without loss of spirituality. Promotes strength
and courage.

Blue Calcite—Assists in accessing a higher frequency of
expression of personal truth. Enhances channeling, toning, and singing.

Blue Lace Agate—Facilitates clear and truthful verbal expression. Promotes self-empowerment through the voice. Stim-

ulates a willingness to express thoughts and feelings, known or unknown.

Carnelian—Activates sexual and procreative energy. Increases vital life force and stimulates creativity. Purifies the blood.

Celestite—Facilitates peaceful strength and mental clarity. Assists in maintaining personal security. Promotes tranquillity and connection to angelic realms. Enhances perception.

Charoite—Clears mental programming of limited thought forms bound by guilt, fear, and the notion of sin. Defuses "the beast." Promotes alignment with soul purpose.

Citrine—Helps manifest personal goals and rebuild self-confidence. Increases alignment of astral bodies. Dissolves feelings of inadequacy. Eases miasmas. Counteracts all forms of radiation poisoning.

Clear Quartz—Assists communication with spirit guides. Expands self-awareness. Helps transform negative thoughts. Alleviates emotional stress.

Cuprite and *Chrysocolla*—Balances male and female powers, which promotes positive relationships. Softens male aggressive tendencies. Helps balance the female reproductive system and menstrual disorders.

Diamond—Master healer that activates attunement to the higher self. Increases the life force and opens the crown chakra.

Emerald—Balances on all levels. Improves relationship with the father. Expands wisdom and projects love. Enhances meditation.

Gold—Master healer. Eases depression and lethargy. Aligns to higher spiritual visions and enlightenment.

Golden Calcite—Integrates spiritual power into earth-plane realities and promotes courage to make necessary changes.

Green Adventurine—Heals on all levels. Soothes conflicts in the emotional body. Eases tension in the solar plexus.

Green Calcite—Aids the transition from old ways of being to new, consciously chosen ones.

Green Smithsonite—Eases fear of interpersonal relationships.

Green Tourmaline—Opens the heart chakra. Eases psychological problems associated with the father.

Hematite—Grounds spiritual energy into and activates the earth star chakra. Balances spiritual energy. Provides psychic and spiritual protection.

Jade—Opens the heart and generates divine love. Grounds the emotions.

Kyanite—Integrates the light body into the mental body. Opèns subtle energy channels and meridians. Promotes new ideas.

Larimar—Connects thoughts with feelings. Empowers. Counteracts depression in young adults. Transmits pure spiritual energy. Promotes peace and tranquillity.

Malachite—Aids left- and right-brain imbalances, epilepsy, dyslexia, autism, and coordination problems. Promotes sleep. Expels plutonium and otherwise detoxifies the system.

Moonstone—Promotes peace and harmony, and pulls toward spiritual things. Enhances psychic development.

Opal (Dark)—Transforms sexual feelings and base emotions into higher expressions. Enhances meditation.

Opal (Light)—Stimulates emotions toward mystical experiences. Opens the solar plexus and brow chakras.

Optical Calcite—Integrates soul star frequency into the crown chakra. Helps access inner knowledge and truth.

Peach Calcite—Transmutes emotional energy into intuitive feelings and insights. Transforms old blocked emotional patterns.

Pearl—Balances emotional extremes. Activates purity, strengthens the body, and stimulates creativity.

Pink Calcite—Enhances unconditional love based on a strong foundation of self-love. Expands the capacity for love and compassion.

Rainbow Hematite—Creates joy in life experiences. Softens the intensity of survival issues. Brings light into the physical plane.

Red Calcite—Activates higher creative forces for new manifestations. Heightens Tantric sexual energies. Helps create vision.

Rose Quartz—Increases the forces of self-love and confidence. Promotes forgiveness and compassion. Balances the lungs and heart.

Ruby—Activates kundalini energy in a balanced fashion. Balances and opens the heart. Provides love and courage to express highest potentials.

Sapphire—Acts as an antidepressant. Stimulates clairvoyance, telepathy, and astral projection. Improves communication with spirit guides.

Selenite—Sends into every cell of the body a message that there is a new way. Assists spirit in finding a home in the body. Transmits the soul frequency.

Silver—Cleanses the subconscious and eases nervous tension, anxiety, and shock.

Topaz—Reverses the aging process and enhances tissue regeneration. Brings out Christ-like qualities.

Turquoise—Master healer. Protects against environmental pollutants. Strengthens the entire anatomy.

WORKING WITH
GEM ESSENCES

*G*em essences act as an interface between the anatomical and etheric levels of the body. They are unique in that they integrate activity on the physiological levels with the energy of the chakras. Individual chakras are energized and balanced through the properties of certain gem essences.

Gem essences can be taken singly or in a program with other gem essences. Starmen Unlimited offers three such programs: Chakra Balancing; Clearing the Physical, Emotional, Mental, and Spiritual Bodies; and Spirit-Body Integration.

C H A K R A   B A L A N C I N G

Humanity's awareness of chakras, centers of energy that exist within our subtle energy bodies, dates back to ancient India and Egypt. The word *chakra* means wheel in Sanskrit, and the chakras are said to resemble whirling vortices of subtle energies.[1] These whirling wheels funnel energy and transmute it into a form the body can use, working as energy transformers from higher to lower frequencies.

Proper functioning of all seven major chakras is crucial to our health since each plays an important role in energizing specific parts of the body. Because each chakra is associated with a particular physiological system, meridian system, and endocrine system, a block in the function of any chakra can result in pathological changes in the nerves, organs, and glands. Conversely, an individual with unblocked chakras can send energy out through them, resulting in higher levels of energy and the ability to have a positive influence on the health and well-being of others.

The existence of chakras has been proven by scientific research. Dr. Hiroshi Motoyama from Japan noted increased energy readings from the chakras of long-term meditators compared with those measured in a control group. He also discovered that some people were able to consciously project energy outward from their chakras.[2] Other researchers have not only verified this effect but also recorded the colors in the aura as well as the predictably measurable energy frequencies associated with each chakra.[3]

In yogic texts, the chakras are described as lotus flowers, with the petals representing the etheric body and the base of the flower, called the nadis, anchored in the physical body. In traditional Eastern understanding, each lotus flower in a relatively unawakened person is hanging down toward the ground. Its energies are then directed downward to sustain survival. When a person meditates and sends energy out, the chakras begin to turn up, sending the energies up the spine. This shift in energy flow is associated with the rise of kundalini energy, which results in higher energetic frequencies, both spiritually and sexually.

The following illustration depicts the seven major chakras, along with their Sanskrit names, qualities and colors connected with them, their light wavelengths, imbalances associated with them, their resonance levels (measured in radio waves), and the endocrine glands they govern.

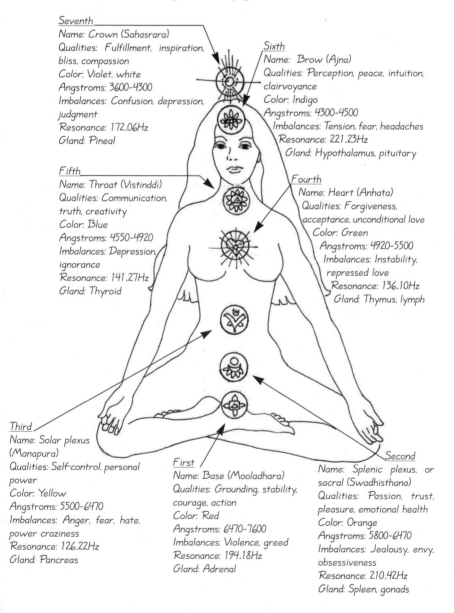

Seventh
Name: Crown (Sahasrara)
Qualities: Fulfillment, inspiration, bliss, compassion
Color: Violet, white
Angstroms: 3600-4300
Imbalances: Confusion, depression, judgment
Resonance: 172.06Hz
Gland: Pineal

Sixth
Name: Brow (Ajna)
Qualities: Perception, peace, intuition, clairvoyance
Color: Indigo
Angstroms: 4300-4500
Imbalances: Tension, fear, headaches
Resonance: 221.23Hz
Gland: Hypothalamus, pituitary

Fifth
Name: Throat (Vistinddi)
Qualities: Communication, truth, creativity
Color: Blue
Angstroms: 4550-4920
Imbalances: Depression, ignorance
Resonance: 141.27Hz
Gland: Thyroid

Fourth
Name: Heart (Anhata)
Qualities: Forgiveness, acceptance, unconditional love
Color: Green
Angstroms: 4920-5500
Imbalances: Instability, repressed love
Resonance: 136.10Hz
Gland: Thymus, lymph

Third
Name: Solar plexus (Manapura)
Qualities: Self-control, personal power
Color: Yellow
Angstroms: 5500-6470
Imbalances: Anger, fear, hate, power craziness
Resonance: 126.22Hz
Gland: Pancreas

First
Name: Base (Mooladhara)
Qualities: Grounding, stability, courage, action
Color: Red
Angstroms: 6470-7600
Imbalances: Violence, greed
Resonance: 194.18Hz
Gland: Adrenal

Second
Name: Splenic plexus, or sacral (Swadhisthana)
Qualities: Passion, trust, pleasure, emotional health
Color: Orange
Angstroms: 5800-6470
Imbalances: Jealousy, envy, obsessiveness
Resonance: 210.42Hz
Gland: Spleen, gonads

FIRST CHAKRA

The first chakra, also known as the base or root chakra, is located at the coccyx, at the bottom of the spinal column. It relates to issues of survival and serves to keep us grounded, or connected to the earth. The root chakra governs the adrenal glands, which secrete adrenaline, the hormone responsible for the fight-or-flight response to danger. When this chakra is not balanced and open, the individual may feel that basic survival issues are being inadequately addressed, most likely resulting in stress. The color associated with this chakra is red, and astrologically it is influenced by our planet Earth and Saturn.

SECOND CHAKRA

The second chakra, also called the sacral chakra or splenic plexus, is located at the sacral nerve plexus in the lower spine—the area that governs sexuality and procreation. Conception is often blocked by preoccupation with survival issues, which indicates a problem in the first chakra.

An imbalance in the second chakra results in either too little or too much sexual energy. Although sexual energy is used to sell us most everything these days, it can be used more wisely, as in some Tantric practices. Awakening the energy of the first and second chakras allows a current to move up through these centers to the heart and higher chakras. This requires balancing and opening all the chakras, resulting in sexual and creative energy expressed through love and understanding. The second chakra is associated with the reproductive organs and the color orange. Astrologically, it is most strongly influenced by the phases of the moon.

T H I R D   C H A K R A

The third chakra is a complex energy center associated with personal power and the ability to manifest that power in the world. Located in the solar plexus, it is the seat of emotions. It is also where energy patterns from past actions and karma from past lives are stored—old emotional energy patterns that decrease our functionality, our ability to resolve difficulties, and our capacity to come into our power. Because we process emotions and relive and resolve past karma in the third chakra, it is important that it be balanced. Otherwise the raw power it contains can manifest as aggression or violence at one extreme or ungrounded etheric energy at the other.

The liver, gallbladder, stomach, pancreas, and small intestine are associated with the third chakra, as is the color yellow. Astrologically, this chakra is most strongly influenced by the sun and the planet Mars.

F O U R T H   C H A K R A

The fourth chakra, the heart chakra, serves as a vital conduit between the lower three chakras and the upper three. Located in the center of the chest, it is connected with love. As energies associated with survival and identity rise up from the first three chakras, they are transmuted into the nonjudgmental energy of love and compassion. Looking at the world through the window of the heart chakra, one sees pure love.

The heart chakra is situated above the province of survival, procreation, and identity issues and below the province of spirit. When there is an ample flow of energy up from the lower three chakras and down from the upper three chakras, the heart chakra is balanced and healthy. The heart and circulatory system are associated with this chakra, which vibrates at the frequency of the color green and is influenced astrologically by Venus.

FIFTH CHAKRA

The fifth chakra, the throat chakra, is the energy center where most human communication is based. Our communication tool, the larynx, is located under this chakra and plays a similar role in transforming energy frequencies, taking the rush of air from wind and transforming it into a vibratory sound and message.

Balancing the fifth chakra requires a flow of energy down from the two upper chakras, which are associated with intuition and spiritual clarity. When the throat chakra is balanced, the individual uses the power of the lower chakras to share love and creative ideas with others. When imbalanced, it can either inhibit the person from speaking up or cause the individual to talk unceasingly. There is often a fine line between being able to speak up for ourselves and having the intuition and spiritual understanding to know when to be silent. Chanting, toning, and singing have powerful balancing effects on the throat chakra, which is associated with the respiratory system and the color blue. Astrologically, it is influenced most by Mercury.

SIXTH CHAKRA

The sixth chakra, known as the brow or third eye chakra, is located in the lower center of the forehead and controls the pituitary system. This energy center conveys the gifts of higher sensing, such as clairvoyance, clairaudience, and intuition, and is associated with the experience of inner light in Eastern religions. According to Indian tradition, the male and female parts of the human body intertwine and twist upward through the first five chakras, merging in the sixth chakra. The Chinese idea of yin and yang describes a similar merging in the sixth chakra.

Imbalance of the sixth chakra can result in depression and unhappiness. It is associated with the color indigo and astrologically is most influenced by Jupiter and Neptune.

S E V E N T H   C H A K R A

The seventh chakra, known as the crown chakra, is located at the top of the head. The Sanskrit name for this energy center, *Sahasrara,* means to multiply by a thousand. The opening of the crown chakra provides an energy flow to the lower chakras and results in an upward flow of spiritual energy into the etheric dimensions that lie beyond personal consciousness.

Before the flow of energy can pass into these dimensions, however, the lower six chakras must be open. It is therefore important to pay special attention to these chakras before addressing whether the crown chakra is balanced, although in most cases this chakra seems to be blocked or closed down rather than out of balance. The pineal gland is associated with this chakra, as is the color violet or white. Astrologically, it is influenced by Uranus.

Kahuna David Bray believed that the lower three chakras are used to bring *mana,* or life force, into the physical body so that the individual can direct it at will. He saw the heart chakra as the place where that energy is transformed into the higher frequencies of love. The heart is also considered the spot where the "crusader" transforms into the "warrior"; whereas crusaders attempt to change the world, warriors try to change themselves, and in so doing, effect a change in the world.[4]

To help systematically energize and balance the seven chakras, Katrina Raphaell assisted Starmen Unlimited in creating a program consisting of seven gem essences. The gems selected were cleansed in the Pacific Ocean on the north coast of Kauai, exposed to lunar and stellar light, and charged at sunrise. We suggest that you begin with gem essences that affect the first chakra and continue with those that influence the second through seventh chakras, spending three days with each essence. The recommended dosage is three to four drops in the mouth two or three times a day. This program should not only balance the chakras but result in a more vital and loving life. A description of the various gem essences in the program and their effects follows.

CHAKRA BALANCING PROGRAM

First chakra. Black tourmaline—Provides psychic protection and grounding for spiritual awareness in the third dimension. Promotes strength.

Second chakra. Carnelian—Activates sexual and procreative energy. Increases vital life force and stimulates creativity.

Third chakra. Citrine—Helps manifest personal goals and rebuild self-confidence. Increases alignment of astral bodies. Dissolves feelings of lack.

Fourth chakra. Green Adventurine and Rose Quartz—Heals on all levels. Soothes conflicts in the emotional body. Eases tension in the solar plexus. Increases the forces of self-love and confidence. Promotes forgiveness and compassion.

Fifth chakra. Blue Lace Agate—Facilitates clear and truthful verbal expression. Promotes self-empowerment through the voice.

Sixth chakra. Amethyst—Enhances mental clarity and strengthens the willpower to break undesirable habits. Calms the mind for meditation.

Seventh chakra. Clear Quartz—Assists communication with spirit guides. Expands self-awareness. Helps transform negative thoughts.

CLEARING THE PHYSICAL, EMOTIONAL, MENTAL, AND SPIRITUAL BODIES

Another program of gem essences offered by Starmen Unlimited is for clearing the four energy bodies. This program was designed to provide a quick means of clearing blockages and patterns, whether from this lifetime or others. The four elixirs, each made up of a combination of two gem essences, can be used either alone or according to a systematic plan to fully clear physical toxins and emotional, mental, and spiritual blockages in the subtle energy bodies. Together, the elixirs cleanse the factors that lead to stress and eventually disease. Because these elixirs are so powerful, we recommend that you monitor the dosage and not take them more than two or three times a day. The following list shows the four types of clearing and, for each one, the recommended elixir and its properties:

Physical clearing. Cuprite and Chrysocolla Elixir—Balances male and female powers, which promotes positive relationships. Softens male aggressive tendencies. Helps balance the female reproductive system and menstrual disorders.

Emotional clearing. Malachite and Green Smithsonite Elixir—Releases suppressed emotions from the solar plexus and improves digestion and breathing. Penetrates and activates hidden emotional patterns and old beliefs.

Mental clearing. Azurite and Larimar Elixir—Penetrates subconscious blocks, enabling greater psychic ability, clearer meditation, and increased mental control.

Spiritual clearing. Charoite and Celestite Elixir—Provides strength and courage to face and dissolve old fears. Evokes peaceful strength and mental clarity. Promotes alignment with soul purpose and highest potential.

SPIRIT-BODY INTEGRATION

Katrina Raphaell, in *The Crystalline Transmission,* presents advanced information on the twelve-chakra system. The twelve chakras were reportedly active in ancient times for a group of people called the Elder race, which had the ability to maintain constant attunement with the energy forces of light radiating from the luminous core of the Mother Milky Way. The information presented by Raphaell provides even more ways to utilize gem essences. She describes a process by which individuals ground and integrate their spiritual light bodies into their physical bodies after the chakras are in balance and the energy bodies have been cleared.

With the guidance of Katrina Raphaell, Starmen Unlimited has created a program of twelve gem essences called Spirit-Body Integration, which can be used after the seven chakras are in balance and the energy bodies are cleared. This integration system is designed to assist in realigning the soul with the body and activating the light body.

The twelve-chakra system includes the seven chakras already discussed plus one chakra in the navel region and four others outside the body. Whereas the Vedic system combines the navel and solar plexus chakras into one, known as the third chakra, in crystal healing each of these centers has its own energy and purpose. The navel chakra is located at the belly button, just below the traditional third chakra. It is the energy center through which divine essence can find human expression in physical manifestation.

The four chakras outside the body include three upper transpersonal energy centers—the stellar gateway chakra, the soul star chakra, and the causal chakra—and one lower center, called the earth star chakra. The stellar gateway chakra is located approximately twelve inches above the top of the head and is the highest chakra that can be incorporated into the human system. As the stellar gateway is opened, the unity of all things can be personally experienced. The state of consciousness it inspires can never be applied to any one individual, as it is the force which is all things.

The soul star chakra is located approximately six inches above the top of the head and is the link between the stellar gateway and the eight human chakras, or the heavens and earth. It translates the infinite energy accessible at the stellar gateway and filters it into the soul level of the human light being. The soul star chakra has the unique ability to assimilate light, and when it is activated, the sense of connection with all things results in a new relationship with the earth.

The causal chakra is located at the center back of the head, approximately three to four inches behind the crown chakra. It is the energy center through which the impersonal divine can manifest in subtle thought patterns. Once the causal chakra is activated and aligned with the soul star, the meaningless thoughts of the mind give way to pure creations originating from the source.

The earth star chakra is located approximately six inches below the soles of the feet. As the earth star is activated, the physical aspects are aligned and attuned to the life-producing force of creation itself. When it is aligned and activated with the upper transpersonal chakras, it weaves golden threads of the impersonal divine into experiences on the earth plane, creating a new fabric of worldly existence.

Starmen Unlimited's Spirit-Body Integration gem elixir program uses different colors of calcite crystals for seven of the chakras; the various calcites link parallel realities and facilitate spiritual understanding of situations that challenge us on the earth plane. Calcite assists in gaining insight into the attraction of particular life circumstances and their spiritual significance.

Selenite, kyanite, and hematite crystals are used to make gem elixirs that work on the upper transpersonal and earth star chakras. A combination of all eleven gem essences, named the Crystalline Transmission, integrates and transmits spiritual energy into all twelve chakras.

The Spirit-Body Integration program is designed to last nearly one month. It is recommended that individuals take three or four drops of one gem essence at a time, two or three times a day for a three-day period. The following is a description of the program:

First chakra (Base chakra). Rainbow Hematite—Creates joy in life experiences. Softens the intensity of survival issues. Brings light into the physical plane.

Second chakra (Sacral chakra). Red Calcite—Activates higher creative forces for new manifestations. Heightens Tantric sexual connections. Helps create vision.

Third chakra (Navel chakra). Golden Calcite—Integrates spiritual power into earth-plane realities and promotes courage to make necessary changes.

Fourth chakra (Solar plexus chakra). Peach Calcite—Transmutes emotional energy into intuitive feelings and insights. Transforms old blocked emotional patterns.

Fifth chakra (Heart chakra). Pink Calcite—Enhances unconditional love based on a strong foundation of self-love. Expands the capacity for love and compassion.

Sixth chakra (Throat chakra). Blue Calcite—Assists in accessing a higher frequency of expression of personal truth. Enhances channeling, toning, and singing.

Seventh chakra (Third eye chakra). Green Calcite—Aids the transition from old ways of being to new, consciously chosen ones.

Eighth chakra (Crown chakra). Optical Calcite—Integrates soul star frequency into the crown chakra. Helps access inner knowledge and truth.

Ninth chakra (Causal chakra). Kyanite—Integrates the light body into the mental body. Opens subtle energy channels and meridians. Promotes new ideas.

Tenth chakra (Soul star chakra). Selenite—Sends into every cell of the body a message that there is a new way. Assists the spirit in finding a home in the body. Transmits the soul frequency.

Eleventh chakra (Earth star chakra). Hematite—Grounds spiritual energy into and activates the earth star chakra. Balances spiritual energy. Provides psychic and spiritual protection.

Twelfth chakra (Stellar gateway chakra). This chakra is not on the material plane and hence cannot be affected by gem essences.

All twelve chakras. Crystalline Transmission—Integrates and transmits spiritual energy into matter as a synthesis of light.

WORKING WITH
FLOWER AND
GEM ESSENCE
COMBINATIONS

*I*n an effort to provide the broadest possible spectrum of products for healing, I consulted the spirit entities that helped me create essences to see whether a combination of flower and gem essences would promote a wider range of healing than individual essences taken alone. I was told they would work together and on multiple levels.

To make sure the combinations Starmen Unlimited produced were based on accurate knowledge, I spent six months researching the uses and properties of most flower and gem essences produced around the world. In addition to getting a thorough education in the essences being used elsewhere, I cataloged and correlated their most common uses. After becoming familiar with the connections between the various essences, I began evaluating the human conditions, patterns, and dysfunctions that were best served through the energies of flowers and gems.

The essences produced by Starmen Unlimited were selected in a methodical manner designed to eliminate any that were not appropriate. The process was the following: I first drew a half-circle, like the upper portion of a clock, and divided it into ten parts. On the left side of the arc I wrote, "0 percent," and on the right, "100 percent." Then, after holding a pendulum motionless over the center of the "clock," I asked the guides to show me what percentage of effectiveness the gem or flower essence in question would have in remedying a specified human condition.

One by one I tested each essence. With every test, the pendulum began motionless and then swung over the arc, providing responses that ranged from 0 percent to 100 percent. All the essences that registered less than 100 percent effective were discarded; the remaining ones had the effectiveness I wanted for the combination remedies.

Next, I sought to find out how the individual essences would work with each other. To discover this, I again asked for the assistance of my spirit guides. Checking the essences in combination resulted in the elimination of those that were not 100 percent effective for a particular purpose, in addition to those that would not work well together.

The blends that passed both these tests were produced as combination remedies, grouped together in various programs—such as Sexuality Enhancers, Preparation for Ascension, Master Ascension—and made available individually as well. When these remedies were viewed via computer-based Kirlian photography by English scientist Harry Oldfield, swirling living patterns could be easily seen within the liquids as well as in the energy fields surrounding the bottled remedies. Interestingly, each remedy had a unique energy signature.

Although the number of different flower or gem essences in each remedy did not seem to be significant in the photographs, clearly different energy levels and patterns were evident in each of them. By contrast, distilled water samples showed none of the elaborate signs of life seen in the remedies. Descriptions of the various programs follow.

SEXUALITY ENHANCERS

Hawaiian flower essences have direct and powerful effects on many aspects of human sexuality, and Hawaiian gem essences associated with the second chakra, the sexual chakra, also play a role in enhancing sexual energies. Hence, combination remedies proved to benefit sexuality in a variety of ways.

The Sexuality Enhancers program was created to address a number of limiting patterns of sexual behavior conditioned by societal attitudes. One of these attitudes is our culture's lack of understanding that sexual energy is a physical expression of spiritual power. In contrast to the manipulative use of sex that often predominates, I believe that the desire to unite sexually with another human being is a reflection of an underlying spiritual need to experience wholeness and oneness.

In my experience, engaging in sexual intercourse solely for the sake of pleasure and instinctual gratification was not enough to satisfy my spiritual nature. It is not surprising, however, that people in our society pursue sex without a spiritual dimension since most forms of advertising utilize sexuality for manipulative purposes. Men are particularly susceptible to using sex manipulatively, because of the pattern of power and dominance over females that for generations has been handed down through patriarchal societies.

Another limiting attitude is our society's lack of support for the notion that all people embody both male and female energies and attributes. Despite the fact that the female is the creative source of every human being, male dominance has repressed the dynamic, soft, and nurturing female energy we all have. The Chinese philosophy of yin and yang reflects the idea that there is both male and female energy in us all, and that biologically we are made up of both our mother's and father's genes. Denying our male or female attributes blocks personal growth as well as spiritual connections in sexual intercourse.

A third limiting attitude is our society's negative social conditioning about the role of sex, resulting in fear of disease, abuse, rape, and other forms of sexual violence. Such conditioning cripples the natural and pleasurable expression of sexuality as well as our ability to love one another. Many religious institutions, for example, stress that sexual intercourse is for creating children, and not for pleasure—an attitude that stems from the view that flesh and spirit are separate. The subconscious confusion and sense of guilt that arise when people believe in such doctrines yet cannot willfully control their sexual desires is extremely damaging, diminishing people's energies and even manifesting as physical disease.

Because the energies of flower and gem essences work on levels of our being that have been blocked and impaired by the stigma of guilt and sin, they play a role in transforming the body's responses during lovemaking. Indeed, Tantric practitioners, who strive to convert these lower patterns into conscious and loving sexual unions, are finding the combination remedies to be invaluable aids.

A final limiting attitude toward sexuality conditioned by our society is the belief that we do not deserve pleasure. The idea that seeking pleasure is selfish and distracting us from more important pursuits causes difficulty in experiencing spiritual pleasure in sexual intercourse and needs to be healed. Graciously receiving love and gifts from others may be the greatest expression of gratitude and respect we can offer them. Communication of this sort eliminates confusion and prompts mutually rewarding experiences. Because such communication can take place only in the present, Tantric practices rely on the smell of incense, the sound of music, the spectacle of dance, and the tactile sensations of massage to bring both partners into the present moment. In that moment, the gift of two spirits merging in the flesh can be given and received.

To address sexuality, Starmen Unlimited has created seven remedies whose powerful effects have been confirmed. Along with taking three or four drops of an essence, I strongly recommend the use of "release statements," which are like affirmations but have a more powerful effect. Affirmations, despite their transformative potential, are self-limiting, because they require individuals to make statements they do not believe; this underlying disbelief weakens the intensity of the affirmation. Instead, it is more effective to make statements releasing certain patterns and ideas that have resulted in energy blockages since there is no problem believing in the existence of such patterns and in the desire to release them. While articulating release statements that you can and do believe, subconscious doubt will not sabotage your efforts.

Of the seven remedies that are available from Starmen Unlimited to enhance various levels of sexual experience, the one that should be used first is Dissolve Sexual Negativity. It is beneficial to begin the Sexuality Enhancers program with this remedy regardless of whether you think it is necessary, since the roots of sexual guilt, conditioning, and confusion go deep and need to be addressed before meaningful progress can take place. The other six remedies can be taken in any order, one at a time for three days, until the program is completed. The following are the remedies, the flower and gem essences used to make them, and suggested release statements.

Dissolve Sexual Negativity—Avocado, Coconut, Haole Koa, Cuprite/Chrysocolla, and Green Smithsonite. "I now release and dissolve my negative conditioning, confusion about sex, and fear of being touched, and rejoice in the divine perfection of my sexuality."

Erotic Lovemaking—Water Lily and Red Calcite. "I now release all sexual limitations and restore my Tantric sexual energies for enriched, erotic, and exciting lovemaking."

Female Sexual Liberator—Hibiscus and Lehua. "I now release my lack of self-esteem and blocked sexual energy patterns, and reclaim balanced and joyful sexual energy."

Male and Female Synergy—Papaya and Red Ginger. "I now release the self-limiting patterns that have denied aspects of my male and female selves, and reunite them in their highest potential."

Male Performance—Banana and Banana Poka. "I now release any imbalances in my sexual energy patterns and open to the rejuvenation of my sexual drive and performance in sexual intercourse."

Men's Sexual Clarity—Spider Lily, Spilanthes, and Sunflower. "I now release my negative beliefs and attitudes about women and temper my male ego to allow higher will and destiny to control my interactions with women."

Sexuality Booster—Water Lily, Basil, Haole Koa, Opal (Dark), Clear Quartz, and Red Calcite. "I now release old attitudes about sexuality that have limited my creative sexual energies, and transform these beliefs to revitalize and enrich my joy in sexuality."

PREPARATION FOR ASCENSION AND MASTER ASCENSION

Ascension is a term used by many people in the New Age movement to mean some form of transformation toward higher frequencies. I see ascension as a completion of a cycle of incarnations and the soul's natural return to the spirit self that seeded its string of lives. Ascension can be viewed as a graduation into godhood by letting go of the lower ego self and becoming the divine soul, a process that entails surrendering your body, mind, and emotions to your real causal self. One possibility is that you would remain in a body that is no longer driven by the ego of the mind and emotions, but rather directed by the infinite love and wisdom of your real self. This practice of letting go is the object of most spiritual, self-transformation, and meditation disciplines.

Letting go can be viewed as being released from the physical body's limitations to a more etheric state. Four spheres constitute the lower astral realms of the universe, while above are the upper causal realms. The first sphere in the lower astral realms is the physical plane; the second is the etheric plane; the third, the emotional plane; and the fourth, the mental plane.

All forms of energy that travel slower than the speed of light belong to the physical plane of the universe. According to some traditions, we are beings from the causal realms who are learning how to live in the physical realm until our physical bodies die, leaving the etheric, emotional, and mental bodies to return to the astral realms. Upon leaving the causal realms, we have penetrated the lower realms, dressing an aspect of our infinite consciousness first in mental energy, then emotional energy, then etheric energy, and finally in physical matter as the baby in our mother's womb. Our physical bodies could be regarded as "space suits" we have donned to enable us to function on this planet.

If we devote ourselves exclusively to things of this world, and give ourselves over to the mind and emotions, then as a result of the laws of karma, or cause and effect, we will have a difficult time working through this incarnation into ascension. Considering the materialism, fantasies, power games, and religious fundamentalism that presently dominate our culture, the struggle to regain our true spiritual identity is analogous to being stuck in a tar pit.

The biggest obstacles to our ascension are the effects of old karma and the presence of fear. Fear, which is the denial that abundance is the nature of life, cuts off our communication with life forms. Fear restrains us so that we are no higher than animals, whose sole aim is basic survival. In addition, fear constitutes the major barrier between us and our innate divinity.

Religions, too, are often barriers to the attaining of our divine identity. After coming into existence to preserve the teachings of their founders, they frequently become corporate institutions whose main reason for existence is their preservation. Toward that end, each religion seeks out new members and competes with others, projecting itself as the

best and only way to God. This cycle has led to war and per-
secution in the name of spiritual virtue, and it is not surprising that ascension is rarely addressed in these religious
traditions.

Interestingly, the word *human* contains the Hawaiian
root word *hu,* which means to rise or gush forth, and a trace
of the word *mana,* which is the divine force or power.
Together they imply that the human purpose is an expression of the divine force.

To ascend in expression of the divine force, we must
transcend time. Rather than live in the lingering illusion of
past experiences, or projections based on memories of them,
we must cut ourselves loose to live fully in the moment. We
need to see time more in terms of the flexibility with which
things interact than as some fixed point or rigid sequence. All
realities actually coexist in the same instant, sharing a common state of timelessness known as the "present." And unless
we are experiencing what is happening in the moment, we
are lost in a sea of dreams composed of memories of pain and
pleasure, and we experience life as empty. Only through
awareness of the moment can we approach the prospect of
moving into higher levels of reality.

Each of us must learn to step away from life's sequence
of events in order to be fully present and participating in the
moment. To better understand this concept, it is helpful to
see energy as divided into countless particles, each an
expression of the One, both in time and space. The principle of the One is a vital key to the attainment of enlightenment as well as ascension. To put it another way, although
every person is a unique expression of God (or life), the
God (or life) we embody is fully One. When we use the
term "God," we ordinarily think of this being as separate or
drastically different from us. We can reverse this pattern by

recognizing that God's consciousness is at all times expressing itself through us, *as* us. God, in other words, is our true self. We are all the One expressing itself in many different ways. Conscious of this dynamic, we become one with All That Is. Such a singular focus is the state many Buddhists, yogis, and aboriginal shamans strive to achieve.

Ultimately, I am committed to the belief that love is the force we must embrace to advance toward a return to our divine state. We have a choice to either commit to that love or dwell in the tar pit of fear. By filling our being with love, no harm can come to us; and through the joyous celebration of life, we will rise to the source.

Starmen Unlimited's two potent flower and gem essence combination programs designed to address issues of ascension are Preparation for Ascension and Master Ascension. The first program serves as a catalyst to resolve issues that stand in the way of a graceful elevation in consciousness. This program will help you overcome addictions and clear negativity by dissolving deep emotional blocks, releasing tension, and providing grounding.

The Master Ascension program includes remedies to connect you with your spirit, attune you to your higher self, align you with divine love, elevate your consciousness, and help you integrate and transmit energy through your twelve chakras. Included is a remedy called Ascension Tension Relief, which releases the natural impatience that can accompany the pursuit of ascension.

Although each individual should be able to intuit and experience the dosage most effective for them, I recommend taking two or three drops no more frequently than three times a day. Each remedy should be taken for three days in any order that feels best. The following are descriptions of the programs, names of the remedies, the flower and gem essences contained in them, and suggested release statements.

PREPARATION FOR ASCENSION PROGRAM

Addiction Detox—Heliconia, Morning Glory, Pua Kenikeni, Christmas Berry, Naio, and Golden Calcite. "I now release the addictive effects of alcohol, food, marijuana, ecstasy, nicotine, opiates, and psychotropic drugs, and I make these changes with courage and love."

Clearing Negativity—African Tulip, Ti, Hila Hila, Naupaka, and Glory Bush. "I now release the effects from all associations with past-life cruelty, dark forces and astral possessions, toxic thoughts of others, and attachment to earthly power, and I give thanks for my liberation."

Deep Emotional Release—Nicotiana, Oleander, Lantana, Kukui, Water Hyacinth, and Peach Calcite. "I now release my sadness, depression, fear, and pain from deeply buried deadened emotions, and choose to transform these old blocked emotions, and I give thanks for my release."

Deep Tension Relief—Yellow Ginger, False Lilac, Orange, Comfrey, and Dandelion. "I now release and dissolve any deep tension and agitating issues from my body, nervous system, and subconscious, and reclaim my peace and power."

Grounding—Lima Bean, Black Tourmaline, Moonstone, and Hematite. "I now release my disconnected, scattered energy patterns and reconnect my spiritual awareness to Mother Earth, and for this I give thanks."

Lighten Up—Zinnia, Marigold, and Rainbow Hematite. "I now release the heaviness of survival issues and embrace the experience of playful joy in a physical body."

Willpower—False Lilac, Mango, Amethyst, and Selenite. "I now release my old lethargy and open to increased mental clarity, strength, and personal power, and I imprint the message on each cell of my body that there is a new way."

M A S T E R   A S C E N S I O N   P R O G R A M

Ascension Tension Relief—Impatiens, Gardenia, and Lemon. "I now release my impatience and intolerance toward accepting what is and embrace the feelings of compassion and peace for myself and all others."

Christ Consciousness—Passion Flower, Topaz, and Jade. "I now release my past lack of spiritual confidence and embrace the spirit of Christ that lives within me."

Consciousness Booster—Passion Flower, Hau, Paka Lana, Lotus, Bougainvillea, and Gold. "I now release the effects of lethargy, powerlessness, depression, and inadequacy, and embrace with confidence the path toward my enlightenment."

Crystalline Transmission—All eleven spirit-body gem essences. "I now release all my energy blocks and integrate and transmit spiritual energy into my twelve chakras as a synthesis of light."

Divine Love—Lime, Passion Flower, Gold, and Pink Calcite. "I now release my lack of confidence in God and my lack of self-love, causing my depression and lethargy, and I attune my consciousness to divine love."

Higher Self Attunement—Canavalia, Lime, Paka Lana, Diamond, and Optical Calcite. "I now release all limitation and attune myself to a permanent connection with my higher self."

Spirit Connection—Angel's Trumpet, Clear Quartz, Sapphire, and Celestite. "I now release the old idea that I am all alone and become open to the loving assistance and guidance of spirit guides, and for this I give thanks."

INDIVIDUAL COMBINATION REMEDIES

In addition to programs, Starmen Unlimited offers individual combination remedies. These remedies, the flower and gem essences contained in them, and the release statements follow:

Addiction Detox—Heliconia, Morning Glory, Pua Kenikeni, Christmas Berry, Naio, and Golden Calcite. "I now release the addictive effects of alcohol, food, marijuana, ecstasy, nicotine, opiates, and psychotropic drugs, and I make these changes with courage and love."

Clearing Negativity—African Tulip, Ti, Hila Hila, Naupaka, and Glory Bush. "I now release the effects from all associations with past-life cruelty, dark forces and astral possessions, toxic thoughts of others, and attachment to earthly power, and I give thanks for my liberation."

Consciousness Booster—Passion Flower, Hau, Paka Lana, Lotus, Bougainvillea, and Gold. "I now release the effects of lethargy, powerlessness, depression, and inadequacy, and embrace with confidence the path toward my enlightenment."

Deep Emotional Release—Nicotiana, Oleander, Lantana, Kukui, Water Hyacinth, and Peach Calcite. "I now release my sadness, depression, fear, and pain from deeply buried deadened emotions, and choose to transform these old blocked emotions, and I give thanks for my release."

Deep Tension Relief—Yellow Ginger, False Lilac, Orange, Comfrey, and Dandelion. "I now release and dissolve any deep tension and agitating issues from my body, nervous system, and subconscious, and reclaim my peace and power."

Dissolve Sexual Negativity—Avocado, Coconut, Haole Koa, Cuprite/Chrysocolla, and Green Smithsonite. "I now release and dissolve my negative conditioning, confusion about sex, and fear of being touched, and rejoice in the divine perfection of my sexuality."

Divine Love—Lime, Passion Flower, Gold, and Pink Calcite. "I now release my lack of confidence in God and my lack of self-love, causing my depression and lethargy, and I attune my consciousness to divine love."

Erotic Lovemaking—Water Lily and Red Calcite. "I now release all sexual limitations and restore my Tantric sexual energies for enriched, erotic, and exciting lovemaking."

Female Sexual Liberator—Hibiscus and Lehua. "I now release my lack of self-esteem and blocked sexual energy patterns, and reclaim balanced and joyful sexual energy."

Grief—Ruby, Dahlia, and Lantana. "I now release the sadness and pain from the emotions of loneliness, abandonment, and loss, and activate love and courage to move on."

Grounding—Lima Bean, Black Tourmaline, Moonstone, and Hematite. "I now release my disconnected, scattered energy patterns and reconnect my spiritual awareness to Mother Earth, and for this I give thanks."

Healing Accelerator—Thyme, Lotus, Comfrey, Diamond, Topaz, Turquoise. "I now release all old blocks that limit my life force energy for healing and reconnect to God for strengthening my entire anatomy, and I give thanks for my healing."

Inspiration—Ruby, Bougainvillea, Lotus, and Azurite. "I now release all old self-limiting patterns and open myself to higher inspiration to express my highest potential, and for this I give thanks."

Less Stress—Hau, Orchid, Wood Rose, Dahlia, Dandelion, Pearl, and Topaz. "I now release my stress and anxiety while activating emotional resiliency and physical stamina."

Life Force Enhancer—Lotus, Lemon, Emerald, Sapphire, Pearl, and Gold. I now release old self-limiting beliefs that have kept me stuck in weak, lethargic, victimized energy patterns and open myself to invigorating accelerated energies, and for this I give thanks."

Love Essence—Charged love-infused formula. "I now release all old energies that keep me in fear of opening my heart in love to myself and others."

Male and Female Synergy—Papaya and Red Ginger. "I now release the self-limiting patterns that have denied aspects of my male and female selves, and reunite them in their highest potential."

Male Performance—Banana and Banana Poka. "I now release any imbalances in my sexual energy patterns and open to the rejuvenation of my sexual drive and performance in sexual intercourse."

Manifesting—Thyme, Bougainvillea, Heliconia, and Emerald. "I now release self-limiting victimized patterns and assimilate new ideas, visions, and inspiration with mental clarity for increased creativity."

Meditation—Lotus, Amethyst, Rosemary, Gold, Turquoise, and Silver. "I now release the mental chatter that distracts me and open to calming, inspired, and peaceful energy, cleansing my subconscious distractions."

Men's Sexual Clarity—Spider Lily, Spilanthes, and Sunflower. "I now release my negative beliefs and attitudes about women and temper my male ego to allow higher will and destiny to control my interactions with women."

Playfulness—Zinnia, Marigold, and Rainbow Hematite. "I now release the heaviness of survival issues and embrace the experience of playfulness and joy in a physical body."

Pregnancy and Labor—Noni, Castor Bean, Moonstone, Amazonite, and Jade. "I now release my fears and anxieties about my pregnancy and labor, and open to energies of calmness and strength."

Regeneration—Lotus, Hau, Thyme, Topaz, and Turquoise. "I now release my belief in the aging process and open to enhanced tissue regeneration and the strengthening of my entire body, mind, and spirit."

Relationship—Geranium, Cuprite/Chrysocolla, Papaya, Basil, Emerald, and Green Smithsonite. "I now release my patterns of fear and mistrust created from past relationships, and open to compassion and understanding in all my relations with others."

Sexuality Booster—Water Lily, Basil, Haole Koa, Opal (Dark), Clear Quartz, and Red Calcite. "I now release old attitudes about sexuality that have limited my creative sexual energies, and transform these beliefs to revitalize and enrich my joy in sexuality."

Shock and Trauma—Lima Bean, Pearl, Ruby, Moonstone, and Silver. "I now release the effects of shock, trauma, anxiety, and tension, and give thanks for my healing."

Spirit Connection—Angel's Trumpet, Clear Quartz, Sapphire, and Celestite. "I now release the old idea that I am all alone and become open to the loving assistance and guidance of spirit guides, and for this I give thanks."

Tranquillity—Naupaka, Rosemary, Turquoise, Opal (Light), and Pearl. "I now release the effects of agitating and destructive momentum in my life, and embrace calmness and peace."

Willpower—False Lilac, Mango, Amethyst, and Selenite. "I now release my old lethargy and open to increased mental clarity, strength, and personal power, and I imprint the message on each cell of my body that there is a new way."

EPILOGUE

Although consensus reality exerts a powerfully hypnotic force on each of us, we continue the struggle to remember our divine essence. Tools like the flower and gem essences offered by Starmen Unlimited are available to assist in this process. Their effect on energetic patterns that keep us in the illusion of being limited helps unlock the door to the true self. I hope you will benefit from them in your journey home.

Another powerful tool for healing is the focused power of our *mana,* or life force. By targeting our flow of mana toward the issues we want to resolve, we can perform "laser surgery" on our psyche and health, and at the same time carry on the wisdom of the Native Hawaiians.

The aloha spirit, another potent force, is one of the healing energies of Hawaii that can be tangibly felt and understood by everyone. In Hawaii *aloha,* the word used for greetings of hello and good-bye, encompasses the concepts of love and compassion. It is therefore not only the property of Hawaiians, but universal in its meaning.

Marcel Vogel, in writing about love, made a statement that aptly sums up the message of this book: "A thought is an act of creation. It is what we are here for, to create, to bring into being ourself by means of thinking. The way a thought can be observed and measured by a simple life form, a plant, shows a wonderful relationship between man and plant. When we love, we release our thought energy and transpose it to the recipient of our love. Our primary responsibility is to love."[1]

Love is the force that we all must embrace in order to return to our divine state. I send you my aloha—my love and compassion—with the hope that the tools in this book will help guide you in the journey to your natural condition of love and joy.

DEVIC ANALYSES
OF
FLOWER ESSENCES

*T*he following section provides devic analyses of twenty-three previously unanalyzed plants growing on Kauai, all of which are included in Starmen Unlimited's essences. These analyses, conducted by Eric Pelham in consultation with the deva of each species, address the the primary healing effects of the plants on the subtle bodies of the human being, illustrating the range of properties a given flower essence may contain. *Note:* All the effects of a particular flower essence may not be appropriate for everyone who tests positive for that essence.

African Tulip
(*Spathodea campanulata*)

African Tulip, a liberating essence, releases afflictions from individuals who have cohabited with lower astral beings in past lives— particularly resultant fears, heaviness, and lack of peace in their present lives. It is especially helpful for those who, having formed an attachment with a dark astral being, underwent a long cohabitation with that being in their astral body. Cohabitations of this sort produce toxins in the astral body in the present life; these act much like physical poisons, causing debilitation and increasing the individual's susceptibility to excessive fears or diseases.

Think of this essence as a cleanser that washes away such toxins, bringing clarity, peace, and freedom from fear, as well as an overall sense of well-being. Because African Tulip acts only on a particular type of astral toxin, it is useful to relatively few people; yet it brings them great relief and much-improved health.

The use of this essence is best guided by higher spiritual beings. Symptoms to look for include extreme restlessness, lack of peace, sudden uncontrollable fears, or recurrent patterns of disease that have no apparent cause.

This essence works by increasing the rate of vibration in the astral body, eliminating toxins that cannot survive such conditions. For permanent results, it must be used over a long period of time. Additional benefits are available when it is used in combination remedies with Ti or Ohelo, which counter the effects of past associations with dark forces. An important tool for redemption, African Tulip can break the deadlock in the recovery process in certain people, facilitating deep healing.

Banana Poka
(Passiflora mollissima)

Banana Poka essence is a balancing and rejuvenating remedy for the male sex drive, the shape of the fruit suggesting its connection with the penis. The chief purpose of this essence is to improve the physical action of the penis in sexual intercourse. In a man with low sex drive, the erection is strengthened, resulting in fuller satisfaction; conversely, in a man with an overactive sex drive, the energy in this area is decreased, leading to more harmonized sexual activity with his female partner. A secondary use of this essence is in preventing the deterioration of bone quality—a minor application compared with its primary function.

This essence works by realigning the penis with the area of the etheric body associated with sexual energy. It has no effect on the brain or third eye, as its action is exclusively physical-etheric. When the essence is taken, the male sexual organ becomes more responsive to and integrated with the sexual energy in the etheric body. Upon further enhancing this area of the etheric body to overcome inertia, any sluggish or disharmonized sexual energies are strengthened and activated. In this way the effects of past misuse of sexual energy can be overcome, and negative energy patterns resulting from the past can be eliminated.

Banana Poka essence is indicated for men who seek adjustment of their sexual energies or improvement of their bone quality, including any attendant psychological problems, such as fear of not performing. It is an energizer for earthly rather than spiritual aspects. Used with other essences, Banana Poka can be a highly beneficial form of sex therapy for men, including those who have committed crimes triggered by excessive sexual energy.

Beach Heliotrope
(Heliotropium curasavicum)

Beach Heliotrope is a comforting essence for children who cry a lot and consequently have trouble breathing, or who often feel sad, victimized, or mistreated. It works best in children up to age twenty-one, because it affects the more juvenile emotions in the emotional body, though it also has a less pronounced effect on adults who are stricken with grief and crying that affects the lungs.

The shape of the flowers and green fruit are symbolic of the function of this essence, since they resemble portions of the lung. Another way in which aspects of this plant mirror its function is in its tendency to grow near salt water, which is reminiscent of tears.

Many children, upon being abused, punished, or mistreated, become choked up with feelings of pain, anguish, or anger, which manifest as tears. At such times, characterized by the blocked state of the emotional body, it becomes harder to breathe evenly or deeply. Beach Heliotrope remedies this problem by realigning the emotions with the soul body, which promotes comfort, and the causal body, which promotes strength. Such realignment stops the flow of excessive tears, comforts the emotions, and strengthens the child to overcome the source of unhappiness. With the rebalancing of the emotional body, breathing deepens, and the child experiences a pervasive sense of calm and well-being, at times even joy.

Beach Heliotrope is a good emergency essence to have on hand in schools, homes, camps, and anywhere else children congregate. It will immediately counter the effects of bullying or abuse, helping to dry up excessive tears while producing an overall state of well-being.

Canavalia
(*Canavalia maritima*)

Canavalia essence helps restore inner radiance and a recognition of priorities at times when they may be obscured. It is a universal essence for individuals unable to establish links with their higher self or maintain their true identity. It works by restoring positive energy to the entire astral body, which can then realign the other subtle bodies. In short, this essence gets people back on track and in touch with their higher self.

One advantage of Canavalia is its versatility. It can be used in a wide variety of situations in which inner light may be diminished as a result of frustration, interference from others, or circumstances throwing the individual off balance. Another positive aspect of Canavalia is the utter simplicity and effectiveness of its action. A single-action remedy, it enhances portions of the astral body that have been separated off because they have become negative. The introduction of positive energy to the astral body invigorates the glow of the aura and helps overcome negative states associated with denial issues.

Canavalia restores inner certainty about one's role in life. As this inner harmony spreads to the other subtle bodies and aligns them, it enhances well-being.

Canna Lily
(*Canna Indica*)

Canna Lily essence heals the heart center in people who have been attacked, abused, or traumatized in a relationship. It helps these individuals overcome hard-heartedness and desire for revenge, promoting instead genuine empathy, caring, and compassion for their abuser. Forgiveness, however, is beyond the action of this essence.

Even though this essence is specifically for survivors of such traumas, it will heal damage to the heart center from abuses in past lifetimes as well. Thus, it has the wonderful capacity to release hard-heartedness resulting from past-life experiences even when the person may not be aware of such a need.

Canna Lily works by energizing the heart center in the astral body. The breakthrough in inertia leads to overcoming a lack of compassion for particular people and situations. This is an excellent essence for people who are undergoing deep healing and rehabilitation, for it restores our true human qualities of love and compassion after circumstances have robbed us of them. Because the enlivening of the heart center is an important prerequisite for deep healing, Canna Lily essence should be a part of emergency combinations given to people in casualty situations. The beautifully colored forms of the flowers represent the sheer loveliness of the heartfelt love and compassion we all need to be truly happy and fulfilled.

Christmas Berry
(*Schinus terebinthfolius*)

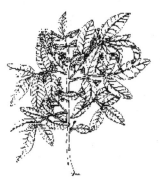

Christmas Berry essence helps individuals recuperate from hangovers caused by alcohol or from the aftereffects of drugs such as the amphetamine MDNA, or ecstasy. The name Christmas Berry alludes to the time of year when frequent intoxication is common, and the aid this essence provides heightens awareness of the true meaning of Christmas—the great festival of divine love. Not only does this essence quickly alleviate the aftereffects of alcohol or certain drugs but it suppresses the desire to use the substance again. It is not, however, a cure for alcohol abuse or ecstasy dependency; it should be viewed instead as an aid to changing patterns of alcohol or drug use and achieving healthier and more meaningful behavior.

Christmas Berry increases the vibrational frequency of the etheric body, enabling it to counteract the condition that alcohol or certain other toxins produce—namely, a cloud that disharmonizes the energy flow. Christmas Berry dispels this cloud, facilitating the harmonious flow of etheric energy. Moreover, once the energy pattern in the cloud is dissolved, there is no tendency for the energy to flow along the same pathway again, and hence the desire to repeat the experience is diminished. By contrast, when a person recovers from a hangover *without* this essence or another healing modality, the energy pattern of the cloud of toxins is maintained, producing a craving to repeat the intoxication experience in order to alleviate the discomfort generated by the energy pattern.

This essence can be used as frequently as needed and is a very good addition to an emergency kit for after-party problems. It is also excellent for use in any long-term detox program that treats alcoholism, ecstasy dependency, or related conditions.

False Lilac
(*Buddleia asiatica*)

False Lilac is an empowering and redemptive essence for individuals who were misused in past lives, particularly those who believed they were doing good but inadvertently stripped others of their personal power and self-respect by acting under the influence of misguided notions. Such individuals in *this* lifetime are powerless in vital ways. Karmically, they must experience the powerlessness they caused others; without personal power, however, they cannot escape the trap of powerlessness. This situation pertains to many people currently in the healing professions.

Thus, individuals who tend to benefit from this essence are aspiring caregivers whose practical ability to assist others is severely limited or constantly thwarted by circumstances. In a past life they may have consigned patients with mental retardation to lunatic asylums or otherwise ruined people's lives by making them powerless victims of a terrible fate. Although these deeds may have been performed with the best of intentions, they produced negative results and contributed to karmic debt.

While it is important to realize that no flower essence can completely eradicate personal karma of this sort, False Lilac will greatly assist people whose karmic debt in this regard is coming to an end. It will also help those in arrears, enabling them to see the issues more clearly and take the steps needed to fulfill their karmic debt.

False Lilac works on the causal body, breaking the deadlock of powerlessness by cleansing the will of toxins resulting from wrong motivation—which restores the will to its proper power and function. Furthermore, it dissolves energy blocks to personal power, which is also located in the causal body. Such blockages were imposed by karmic angels to prevent the individuals from accessing full personal power in their present lifetime. Thus, this essence has a dual action: it cleanses the will and simultaneously restores personal power as well as the ability to control individual destiny.

Glory Bush
(Tibouchina urvilleana)

Glory Bush is a healing, peace-inducing essence for individuals who in past lives aroused fear in others by ritualistic means, mainly in tribal societies. It is especially helpful for those suffering from the karmic outcomes associated with provoking this type of fear.

The immediate effect of Glory Bush is tangible relaxation as the fear and pain held in the heart chakra are relieved. A deeper effect takes place in the psyche, however, where paranoia will give way to peace and understanding. This essence acts to literally redeem suffering that is karmically linked to distress inflicted on others in past lives. Although it cannot shortcut karma by circumventing one's allotment of suffering, it can accelerate the healing of the underlying issues.

Glory Bush essence has a profound effect on people experiencing inner turmoil and many types of karmic suffering, bringing relaxation and deep peace. It works by enhancing the astral body in such a way as to overcome negativity within the psyche. By relieving such negativity, it reduces inner conflict and paranoia. This essence provides the most benefits in regression work and past-life healing.

Golden Amaranth
(*Amaranthus spinosus*)

Golden Amaranth strengthens the immune system to prevent viral infections associated with the solar plexus area and the intestines, such as viral hepatitis; gastroenteritis; Bornholm disease; hand, foot, and mouth disease; and some types of dysentery. It is important to realize that this essence is for disease prevention, not remediation. Nevertheless, if you already have any of these diseases, then Golden Amaranth can greatly aid the later stages of recovery by building up the immune system. Please note that although this essence will boost the immune response to viral infections in *other* parts of the body, it will not provide immunity against bacteria or HIV infections.

Golden Amaranth essence increases the health of the immune system by augmenting the life force coming from the astral body to the solar plexus chakra. It also improves the astral body's alignment with the physical body, promoting increased balance and harmony in the solar plexus area and nearby intestines and thereby guarding against invading viruses.

Golden Amaranth can also be used as part of a general booster before visiting areas of the world that are rife with viral diseases affecting the solar plexus area, such as hepatitis in India. It will improve overall health and specifically protect against such viruses.

Gomphrena-bozo
(*Gomphrena globosa*)

Gomphrena, known as the diplomat's essence, facilitates mental and emotional sensitivity to Native people. It is especially useful in preventing conflict and misunderstanding if individuals traveling to a foreign country will be playing a dominant role with respect to the indigenous people. On the one hand, although this essence acts on any invading force, it is perhaps most directly applicable to international travelers and businesspeople seeking to obtain resources or raw materials, such as oil company personnel. On the other hand, as it provides rapid adaptation to an unfamiliar culture, it is useful for *all* people traveling overseas.

Gomphrena works by stimulating harmony in thought, attuning the mental body to the new situation. Moreover, it dissolves preconditioned emotional blocks that manifest as hostility, coldness, negativity, or lack of care. This aspect of the essence is most profound since interactions with people of other cultures take place on an emotional rather than on a mental or physical level, particularly when communication barriers are present. Good feelings toward people of another culture can overcome virtually any problem, whereas bad feelings make all interactions difficult. Thus, Gomphrena can be of considerable use to many people.

Haole Koa
(Leucaena latisiliqua)

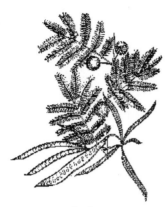 Haole Koa is a liberating essence for individuals who, under the influence of a group, have been sexually repressed or negatively conditioned with regard to sexuality. It harmonizes the mental body by raising its vibration, enabling it to overcome negativity toward sex; in this way it revitalizes the flow of sexual energies in the body and restores wholesome attitudes toward sex without necessarily changing sexual activity. It also dissolves energy blockages in the area of the etheric body connected with sex, thus releasing constrictions in the flow of sexual energy and helping it come to healthy expression once again.

Haole Koa is useful for people who, conditioned by dogma, believe that sex is wrong, or sinful, and who therefore feel guilty about expressing their sexual energy. It also helps individuals who have sexual perversions and associate sex with violence, animals, children, or pain. In addition, it assists couples experiencing difficulty with sexual performance or fulfillment due to strong negative programming that is blocking sexual expression.

Haole Koa helps people reassess their psychological approach to sex, enabling them to view it as wholesome, good, healthy, and desirable, while simultaneously revitalizing and liberating sexual energies. It works equally well for people of any age and gender, and is especially valuable to individuals who are undergoing a change of lifestyle regarding their sexuality, such as a renunciation of celibacy. Despite the many areas of application for Haole Koa, it only affects conditioning that has been influenced by a group rather than an individual.

Hila Hila
(*Mimosa pudica L.*)

Hila Hila, a transformational essence for the consciousness, helps convert derogatory thoughts of others into loving ones and allows individuals to see others as equal to themselves. This essence is for people who cannot stop thinking disparagingly about others and perceiving themselves as superior, regardless of the good intentions they may have.

Such dynamics are often triggered by false pride or by a dark side that projects itself onto others. In either instance, when individuals can no longer see themselves on equal terms with others, their minds begin to compartmentalize—that is, the mind starts to see itself only in relation to others. This separation of the mind is responsible for many of the negative thoughts that prompt disharmonious action in human affairs. When the mind is whole, on the other hand, positive, holistic thoughts and attitudes prevail.

Hila Hila is a divine essence that brings us back to this natural state of mental wholeness through its cleansing action. It vibrates away toxic thoughts by introducing clear, harmonic energy into the mental body. As the disharmonious thought energy is eliminated, positive, loving thoughts emerge.

People with varying degrees of negative thoughts about others can benefit from this essence. It will work on mildly unpleasant thoughts as well as highly contemptible ones—most of which lie in the psyche, where they well up from unresolved conflicts carried over from past lives. Over time, it can deepen one's insights into all human interactions.

Lantana
(Lantana camara L.)

Lantana essence helps to harmonize conflicting emotions, allowing for a fuller release of sadness or pain through crying. Although it does not cause crying, it facilities healing after tears have started to flow. When a person cries to release sadness or pain, the process of healing is often disrupted by the mind or will, which inhibits the release of emotions through tears, ultimately giving rise to conflict.

Lantana essence, in acting to harmonize the emotions, unifies and integrates the emotional body, increasing the release of tears. In the process, it severely reduces the ability of the mental or causal body to dissipate this emotional release, resulting in greater comfort and optimal benefits.

Depending on individual needs, Lantana can be used with excellent outcomes in combination with other essences that help to release emotions through tears, such as the Australian Sturt Desert Pea or the Indian essence Ashoka.

Mock Orange

(Murraya exotica)

Mock Orange, a valuable energizing and resensitizing essence for the nervous system, can be used in a number of specific situations. It can aid recuperation after an illness; help people who are out of step with others, such as those with learning difficulties; and revitalize the nervous system after overwork, stress, or trauma. Moreover, it can help awaken sensuality and magic in the lives of people who have been through difficult times, or of children who have never known real sensitivity. Because it stimulates only the nervous system, not the emotions (like Bougainvillea), it benefits the physical senses.

Mock Orange can be used as a pick-me-up for faculties of perception when needed and also as a long-term aid in countering dullness, lethargy, or insensitivity resulting from any cause. It produces a state of energetic sensitivity, promoting a quickness and subtlety of response to others. Since it can make a person more sensitive to energy states and needs, it will enhance relationships with others.

This essence works by realigning the nervous system in the etheric body with the astral body, increasing the energy going into the senses and into nervous responsiveness. Because its action is self-adjusting, it will not overstimulate individuals whose nervous systems are already highly energized.

Morning Glory
(*Ipomea purpurea*)

All varieties of Morning Glory essences liberate individuals from certain types of substance abuse while revitalizing the nervous system. Used as part of an integrated program, they can help people overcome addictions to such drugs as tobacco and opiates, and heal their etheric body so that they no longer desire these substances. They do not, however, work on all classes of drugs, notably alcohol and hallucinogens. There is also a wider application of Morning Glory essence—to aid many types of nervous system disequilibrium, such as itchy insect bites, lack of sleep due to nervous tension and instability, and general malaise.

Morning Glory works by first realigning the etheric body with the astral body, stimulating the astral body to restore proper equilibrium to the nervous system. It acts further by helping the etheric body overcome negative energy states that drugs like nicotine and opiates produce. The combination of these two actions revitalizes people who have compromised the quality of their nervous systems through use of these drugs, enhances the quality of nervous energy flow, and restores well-being.

Naupaka Kuahiwi
(Beach Naupaka; *Scaevola gaudichaudiana*)
Naupaka Kahakai
(Mountain Naupaka; *Scaevola taccada*)

Both Beach Naupaka and Mountain Naupaka essences alleviate mental negativity concerning dreams, beliefs in reincarnation, and other spiritual matters. These essences are for people attached to earthly power or to the pursuit of glamour or wealth, to whatever degree these tendencies manifest. Because such tendencies are often built up over many lifetimes, getting stronger with each one, individuals who become attached to them are inclined to vigorously deny the existence of an afterlife and of spiritual responsibility for their earthly actions. They use their will to sever the conscious connection between their earthly mind and their higher self, abdicating their true responsibilities on earth. When the conscience is put to sleep from such disregard, energy is withdrawn from it. As a result, the lessons and events of dreams become detached from the conscious mind, and this energy goes instead toward the pursuit of earthly power.

Naupaka essences overcome hostility toward spiritual matters and other forms of mental negativity by encouraging the energy in the mental body to vibrate at a higher frequency and by strengthening the alignment of the mental body with the astral body. Simultaneously, they reconnect the conscious mind to important life issues and fundamental knowledge stored in the astral body. Thus, individuals become concerned with more profound life issues and real responsibilities toward themselves and others. Use of these essences over time corrects many imbalances acquired as a result of earthly life, enabling individuals to experience fulfillment.

A truly balanced Naupaka essence contains flowers from both Beach and Mountain species; the Naupaka flower essence available from Starmen Unlimited contains one-half of each variety. Because the flowers of the Beach and Mountain varieties resemble two halves of one flower, this blend symbolizes solidarity between the need to find fulfillment and happiness on earth (along the beaches) and the need to reunite with the higher self (on the mountaintops). We like to think of our essence as the reuniting of lovers, a notion that reflects an old Hawaiian myth about two lovers separated by a jealous deity. According to this myth, the male was sent to the mountains and lives today through the Mountain Naupaka, while the female was imprisoned by the seashore as the Beach Naupaka. Put together, the two varieties make a whole.

Paka Lana
(*Telosma cordata*)

Paka Lana essence is a restorative remedy to help reestablish an inner space that conveys perfect peace and a true sense of proportion. It is intended especially for the advanced lightworker whose progress in spiritual work has been hampered by earthly disharmonies and whose inner peace and sense of proportion have been compromised. It works on the highest vibrations within the self to restore the clear direction of inner light, enhancing the soul body to overcome disharmony so that all its aspects assume their proper relationship to one another. It does this by untangling light fibers in the soul body that have become entangled and by reestablishing a resonant harmony among aspects that have become fused together. This action creates peace and proportion in an individual's consciousness.

The demands of physical life can so warp human judgment and motivation that one's inner peace and sense of proportion become threatened. The resulting anxiety can be aggravating, especially to individuals who have incarnated specifically to bring a high energy or consciousness to the earth, for then they cannot progress in their mission. In such circumstances, Paka Lana can reestablish the space of inner peace and correct proportion.

This essence is useful as an aid to meditation and is of benefit to individuals who work in advanced healing or engage in other spiritual pursuits, as well as initiates on the spiritual path who are trying to determine their true identity. One of the very high spiritual essences from the Hawaiian Islands, Paka Lana is a lovely blessing and a gift from God.

Shower Tree
(*Cassia javanica L.*)

Shower Tree essence promotes peace among people of different cultures by alleviating suspicion and dissolving barriers to understanding. It hastens universal brotherhood among those who employ different languages or concepts because it immediately defuses the biggest obstacle to communication—fear. This essence is helpful in a wide range of situations that appear to have no common ground in cross-cultural relations. It can also help alleviate fear in relationships between culturally and linguistically similar people with markedly different mind-sets, because it produces a state of warm regard, flexibility of mind, and openness to learning.

Shower Tree essence can be used as a preventive remedy to help ensure that conflict between people of different cultures does not occur. It is also useful in reestablishing peace after conflict and acrimony, although in these circumstances it is best used with forgiveness-type essences.

Shower Tree works by dissolving blocks in the mental body related to comprehension of other cultures and languages, thus reducing rigidity and defeatist attitudes, and improving mental flexibility and willingness to learn. It also dissolves blocks in the astral body, dissipating fears and apprehension and bringing peace, love, and openness. Overall, this essence promotes a wonderful combination of energies to facilitate even the most difficult encounters with strangers.

Spilanthes
(*Spilanthes acmella*)

Spilanthes essence is especially for men who need to resolve confusion or conflict regarding the appropriateness of a partner, both sexually and in terms of other aspects of compatibility. It is most useful in situations involving a very attractive or sexually desirable female who may interest a number of men, leading to potential or actual conflict. It helps men control their sexual energy, allowing them to clearly and honestly decide whether or not they are sexually compatible with particular women. This remedy, however, is not effective for women.

Spilanthes works by realigning the sexual energies in the etheric body with the higher will and destiny, which is located in the causal body. The higher will is then made manifest to the consciousness, where it can control the movement and orientation of sexual energies. Since all subtle bodies affect all other subtle bodies, the demonstration of the higher will controlling sexual energy in an appropriate way reveals to the mind and emotions clarification regarding relationship issues. In other words, clarity in one subtle body will produce clarity in the others by a resonance interaction.

Although Spilanthes can benefit almost any man at some stage of life, especially when he is unsure about whether he should be with a particular woman, it is an important essence for young adolescent males or highly sexed men with a proclivity for dominant behaviors or sexual promiscuity. It is particularly geared to macho societies in which men may believe that they own women and therefore need not pay attention to male-female compatibility.

Vervain
(*Verbenaceae*)

 Vervain is a relaxant for people with a high degree of nervous tension. It balances and harmonizes the nervous system so that energy flows through it smoothly and nervous stress and tension are alleviated. It acts pure-

ly on the etheric body, and hence has no direct influence on mental tension, although some relief from this condition may occur as a secondary effect.

This is a universal essence that can be used for numerous purposes by a wide variety of people. It is, for example, an excellent relaxant to facilitate sleep among individuals who have been engaged in an activity that produces nervous stress and tension. It is also soothing before plane travel for individuals who react nervously to flying. Although people who are high-strung and suffer from nervous tension are obvious candidates for this essence, anyone suffering from nervous stress or tension can benefit from it.

Vervain has no physical effects—it does not act on the lymphatic system, for example—although a secondary gain is sometimes experienced in a subtle body complementary to the one acted upon. The reason there is very little resonance effect on the physical body is that the "wave form" of this remedy is closely tailored to the nervous system, which is situated in the etheric body and is controlled from the astral body. Vervain essence works because the astral body is the coordination center of all the subtle bodies, and nervous tension is the result of poor energy flow in a part of the etheric body. Through selective realignment with the etheric body, the astral body is restored, and energy blockages or impediments are eliminated. In this way Vervain helps to balance energy and solve problems of nervous tension.

Water Hyacinth
(*Eichhornia crassipes*)

Water Hyacinth essence cleanses the emotions in individuals who build up heavy, congested feelings during the winter months or any extended period of time free of sunlight. As a result of its action, depression, fear, apprehension, and heaviness are lifted, leaving people feeling light, optimistic, and positive about themselves and life in general. It is also for anyone who has built up depressed feelings while undergoing a difficult period in life. In short, it rids people of an accumulation of heavy, negative, and toxic emotions. Being a water flower, it enhances the flow of life and the moving sea of feelings with its renewing properties.

Interestingly, Water Hyacinth is a popular winter flower in many countries because of its ability to cleanse emotional "garbage" from the aura, which tends to accumulate in winter. This lovely universal antidepressant and emotional cleanser not only alleviates the winter blues and aids recovery from difficult periods of life but also helps people overcome negative attitudes toward others.

Water Hyacinth works by eliminating from the emotional body toxic emotions that have accumulated over a period of time. It produces a light, calm, and positive state of mind and emotions, and is a blessing to all who are adversely affected by lack of sun.

Wood Rose

(Ipomoea tuberosa)

 Wood Rose essence relaxes nervous tension in people who work too hard. It is especially suited for individuals who live with great pressures and responsibilities and find it hard to fully relax because of accumulation of fear in the psyche, although it will help reduce any type of nervous tension. It is a revitalizing tonic for the parasympathetic nervous system, and it works by harmonizing the astral body to overcome fear.

Although many people suffering from nervous stress and tension can benefit from this essence, its greatest effect is on those who carry fear—especially fear of losing a job, of unpopularity, of the unknown, or of not succeeding. Since it works best on nervous tension connected with overwork, the fears it alleviates tend to be work related.

Wood Rose is a relative of Morning Glory, which also affects the nervous system, and its yellow flower represents the sun, which dispels all fear. It works by dissolving blockages in the etheric body and enhancing the astral body to overcome the disharmony produced by fear. Since the astral body is the central integration point, this remedy has a marked harmonizing and balancing effect on the entire individual, eliminating stress and promoting well-being.

N O T E S

Chapter 3
1. Serge Kahili King, *Mastering Your Hidden Self* (Wheaton, IL: The Theosophical Publishing House, 1985), pp. 10–11.
2. Isabella Arona Abbott, *La'au Hawai'i: Traditional Hawaiian Uses of Plants* (Honolulu, HI: Bishop Museum Press, 1992), p. 98.
3. Max Freedom Long, *The Secret Science at Work* (Marina del Rey, CA: DeVorss & Company, 1953), p. 123.
4. Max Freedom Long, *The Secret Science behind Miracles* (Marina del Rey, CA: DeVorss & Company, 1991), p. 34.
5. David K. Bray and Douglas Low, *The Kahuna Religion of Hawaii,* ed. by Riley Hansard Crabb (Vista, CA: Borderline Sciences Research Foundation, 1980), p. 10.
6. David Malo, *Hawaiian Antiquities* (Honolulu, HI: Bishop Museum Press, 1898), p. 81.
7. June Gutmanis, *Na Pule Kahiko* (Honolulu, HI: Editions Limited, 1983), pp. 4–5, fn. 7.
8. Ibid., p. 6, fn. 11.
9. Ibid., p. 6, fn. 12.
10. Ibid., p. 6.
11. Ibid., p. 14.
12. Scott Cunningham, *Hawaiian Religion and Magic* (St. Paul, MN: Llewellyn Publications, 1994), pp. 54–55.
13. See Note 7, p. 15.
14. Ibid., p. 30.
15. St. John 1:1, 1:14. Bible, King James Version.
16. Genesis 1:3, 1:9. Bible, King James Version.
17. See Note 3.
18. See Note 3, p. 141.
19. Craighill Handy et al., "Outline of Hawaiian Physical Therapeutics," *B. P. Bishop Museum Bulletin* 126 (1934): 1–52.
20. See Note 3.
21. Marie C. Neal, *In Gardens of Hawaii* (Honolulu, HI: Bishop Museum Press, 1948), p. 625.

Chapter 4

1. George De La Warr and Douglas Baker, *Biomagnetism* (Oxford, England: De La Warr, 1967).
2. Franklin Loehr, *The Power of Prayer on Plants* (New York: Signet Books, 1969).
3. Robert N. Miller, "The Positive Effect of Prayer on Plants," *Psychic* (April 1972): 24–25.
4. Thomas E. Oxman, MD, et al., "Lack of Social Participation or Religious Strength and Comfort As Risk Factors after Cardiac Surgery in the Elderly," *Psychosomatic Medicine* 57 (1995): 5–15.
5. Claudia Wallis, "Faith and Healing: Can Prayer, Faith and Spirituality Really Improve Your Physical Health?" *Time* (24 June 1996): 58.
6. Ibid.
7. Ibid.
8. Herbert Benson, *Timeless Healing: The Power and Biology of Belief* (New York: Scribner, 1966).
9. Richard Gerber, *Vibrational Medicine* (Santa Fe, NM: Bear & Company, 1981), p. 286.
10. Aubrey Westlake, "Vis Medicatrix Naturai," *Proceedings of the Scientific and Technical Congress of Radionics and Radiesthesia* (May 1950).
11. Bernard Grad, "A Telekinetic Effect on Plant Growth," *International Journal of Parapsychology* 5, no. 2 (1963): 117–133.
12. Bernard Grad, "An Unorthodox Method of Treatment on Wound Healing in Mice," *International Journal of Parapsychology* 3 (Spring 1961): 5–24.
13. Dolores Krieger, "The Response of In-Vivo Human Hemoglobin to an Active Healing Therapy by Direct Laying On of Hands," *Human Dimensions* 1 (Autumn 1972): 12–15.
14. Dolores Krieger, "Therapeutic Touch: The Imprimatur of Nursing," *American Journal of Nursing* 75 (1975): 784–787.
15. André Bovis, Pamplets on dowsing (Nice, France: privately printed, 1930–1945).
16. Robert Miller, "Methods of Detecting and Measuring Healing Energies," in *Future Science,* ed. by White and Rippner (Garden City, NY: Doubleday & Company, 1977), pp. 431–444.
17. Cleve Backster, "Evidence of a Primary Perception in Plant Life," *International Journal of Parapsychology* 10, no. 4 (Winter 1968): 329–348.
18. V. N. Pushkin, "Flower Recall," *Znaniya Sila* (November 1972).
19. Peter Tompkins and Christopher Bird, *Secret Life of Plants* (New York: Harper & Row, 1973), pp. 23–24.

Chapter 5
1. T. Moss, "Puzzles and Promises," *Osteopathic Physician* (February 1976): 30–37.
2. I. Dumitrescu, "Life Energy Patterns Visible via New Technique," *Brain/Mind Bulletin* 7, no. 14 (23 August 1982).
3. Machaelle Small Wright, *Dancing in the Shadows of the Moon* (Warrenton, VA: Perlandra, Ltd., 1995), p. 11.
4. Michael J. Roads, *Talking with Nature* (Tiburon, CA: H. J. Kramer, 1985), p. 34.
5. Arthur D. Culler, *The Poetry of Tennyson* (New Haven, CT: Yale University Press, 1977).
6. Matthew 6:28. Bible, Revised Standard Version.
7. Serge Kahili King, *Kahuna Healing* (Wheaton, IL: The Theosophical Publishing House, 1983), p. 114.
8. Myrna I. Lewis and Robert N. Butler, MD, *Sex after Sixty* (Boston: Hall, 1977).
9. Edward Bach, "Heal Thyself," in *The Bach Flower Remedies* (New Canaan, CT: Keats Publishing Company, 1977).
10. Arthur E. White, ed., *The Hermetical and Alchemical Writings of Paracelsus,* vol. 2 (Boulder, Co: Shambhala Publications, 1976), pp. 304–305.
11. Gurudas, *Flower Essences and Vibrational Healing* (San Rafael, CA: Cassandra Press, 1983), pp. 7–8.
12. Edward Bach, *Heal Thyself* (Ashington, Rochford, Essex, England: C. W. Daniel Co., Ltd., 1931), pp. 45–47.

Chapter 6
1. Peter Tompkins and Christopher Bird, *Secret Life of Plants* (New York: Harper & Row, 1973), pp. 312–313.

Chapter 7
1. Gurudas, *Gem Elixirs and Vibrational Healing,* vol. 1 (San Rafael, CA: Cassandra Press, 1985), p. 33.

Chapter 8
1. Charles Webster Leadbeater, *The Chakras* (Wheaton, IL: Theosophical Publishing House, 1977).
2. Hiroshi Motoyama and R. Brown, *Science and the Evolution of Consciousness: Chakras, Ki and Psi* (Brookline, MA: Autumn Press, Inc., 1978), pp. 93–98.
3. Valerie Hunt, "Electronic Evidence of Auras: Chakras in UCLA Study," *Brain/Mind Bulletin* 3, no. 9 (20 March 1978).
4. David K. Bray and Douglas Low, *The Kahuna Religion of*

Hawaii, ed. by Riley Hansard Crabb (Vista, CA: Borderland Sciences Research Foundation, 1980).

Epilogue
1. Marcel Vogel, cited in Robert Miller, "The Healing Magic of Crystals: An Interview with Marcel Vogel," *Science of Mind* (August 1984).

BIBLIOGRAPHY

Abbott, Isabella Arona. *La'au Hawai'i: Traditional Hawaiian Uses of Plants.* Honolulu, HI: Bishop Museum Press, 1992.

Bach, Edward. "Heal Thyself." In *The Bach Flower Remedies.* New Canaan, CT: Keats Publishing Company, 1977.

Backster, Cleve. "Evidence of a Primary Perception in Plant Life." *International Journal of Parapsychology* 10, no. 4 (Winter 1968): 329–348.

Benson, Herbert. *Timeless Healing: The Power and Biology of Belief.* New York: Scribner, 1966.

Bovis, André. Pamphlets on dowsing. Nice, France: privately printed, 1930–1945.

Bray, David K., and Douglas Low. *The Kahuna Religion of Hawaii.* Edited by Riley Hansard Crabb. Vista, CA: Borderline Sciences Research Foundation, 1980.

Culler, Arthur D. *The Poetry of Tennyson.* New Haven, CT: Yale University Press, 1977.

Cunningham, Scott. *Hawaiian Religion and Magic.* St. Paul, MN: Llewellyn Publications, 1994.

Dumitrescu, I. "Life Energy Patterns Visible via New Technique." *Brain/Mind Bulletin* 7, no. 14 (23 August 1982).

Gerber, Richard. *Vibrational Medicine.* Santa Fe, NM: Bear & Company, 1981.

Grad, Bernard. "A Telekinetic Effect on Plant Growth." *International Journal of Parapsychology* 5, no. 2 (1963): 117–133.

_____, et al. "An Unorthodox Method of Treatment on Wound Healing in Mice." *International Journal of Parapsychology* 3 (Spring 1961): 5–24.

Gurudas. *Flower Essences and Vibrational Healing.* San Rafael, CA: Cassandra Press, 1983.

_____. *Gem Elixirs and Vibrational Healing,* vol. 1. San Rafael, CA: Cassandra Press, 1985.

Gutmanis, June. *Na Pule Kahiko.* Honolulu, HI: Editions Limited, 1983.

Handy, Craighill, et al. "Outline of Hawaiian Physical Therapeutics." *B. P. Bishop Museum Bulletin* 126 (1934): 1–52.

Hunt, Valerie. "Electronic Evidence of Auras: Chakras in UCLA Study." *Brain/Mind Bulletin* 3, no. 9 (20 March 1978).

King, Serge Kahili. *Kahuna Healing.* Wheaton, IL: The Theosophical Publishing House, 1983.

————. *Mastering Your Hidden Self.* Wheaton, IL: The Theosophical Publishing House, 1985.

Krieger, Dolores. "The Response of In-Vivo Human Hemoglobin to an Active Healing Therapy by Direct Laying On of Hands." *Human Dimensions* 1 (Autumn 1972): 12–15.

————. "Therapeutic Touch: The Imprimatur of Nursing." *American Journal of Nursing* 75 (1975).

Leadbeater, Charles Webster. *The Chakras.* Wheaton, IL: The Theosophical Publishing House, 1977.

Lewis, Myrna I., and Robert N. Butler, MD. *Sex after Sixty.* Boston: Hall, 1977.

Loehr, Franklin. *The Power of Prayer on Plants.* New York: Signet Books, 1969.

Long, Max Freedom. *The Secret Science at Work.* Marina del Rey, CA: DeVorss & Company, 1953.

————. *The Secret Science behind Miracles.* Marina del Rey, CA: DeVorss & Company, 1991.

Malo, David. *Hawaiian Antiquities.* Honolulu, HI: Bishop Museum Press, 1898.

Miller, Robert N. "The Healing Magic of Crystals: An Interview with Marcel Vogel." *Science of Mind* (August 1984).

————. "Methods of Detecting and Measuring Healing Energies." In *Future Science.* Edited by White and Rippner. Garden City, NY: Doubleday & Company, 1977.

————. "The Positive Effect of Prayer on Plants." *Psychic* (April 1972): 24–25.

Moss, T. "Puzzles and Promises." *Osteopathic Physician* (February 1976): 30–37.

Motoyama, Hiroshi, and R. Brown. *Science and the Evolution of Consciousness: Chakras, Ki and Psi.* Brookline, MA: Autumn Press, Inc., 1978.

Neal, Marie C., *In Gardens of Hawaii.* Honolulu, HI: Bishop Museum Press, 1948.

Oxman, Thomas E., MD, et al. "Lack of Social Participation or

Religious Strength and Comfort As Risk Factors after Cardiac
    Surgery in the Elderly." *Psychosomatic Medicine* 57 (1995): 5–15.

Pushkin, V. N. "Flower Recall." *Znaniya Sila* (November 1972).

Raphaell, Katrina. *Crystal Enlightenment.* Santa Fe, NM: Aurora
    Press, 1985.

_____. *Crystal Healing.* Santa Fe, NM: Aurora Press, 1987.

_____. *The Crystalline Transmission.* Santa Fe, NM: Aurora Press,
    1990.

Roads, Michael J. *Talking with Nature.* Tiburon, CA: H. J. Kramer,
    1985.

Tompkins, Peter, and Christopher Bird. *Secret Life of Plants.* New
    York: Harper & Row, 1973.

Wallis, Claudia. "Faith and Healing: Can Prayer, Faith and
    Spirituality Really Improve Your Physical Health?" *Time* (24
    June 1996): 58.

Warr, George De La, and Douglas Baker. *Biomagnetism.* Oxford,
    England: De La Warr, 1967.

Westlake, Aubrey. "Vis Medicatrix Naturai." *Proceedings of the
    Scientific and Technical Congress of Radionics and Radiesthesia*
    (May 1950).

White, Arthur E., ed. *The Hermetical and Alchemical Writings of
    Paracelsus,* vol. 2. Boulder, CO: Shambhala Publications, 1976.

Wright, Machaelle Small. *Dancing in the Shadows of the Moon.*
    Warrenton, VA: Perlandra, Ltd., 1995.

ABOUT THE AUTHOR

Ken Carlson has lived in Hawaii for more than a decade. He originally came to Kauai as an environmental lawyer and has since dedicated his life to personal and planetary healing through the creation of Hawaiian flower and gem essence remedies.

O R D E R   F O R M

Quantity	*Item*	*Amount*
_____	*Star Mana: The Healing Energies of Hawaii* ($14.00)	_____
_____	Star Mana Travel Kit: ⅛-ounce bottles of Deep Tension Relief, Grounding, Healing Accelerator, Life Force Enhancer, Manifesting, Meditation, Playfulness, and Shock & Trauma ($32.00)	_____
	Sales tax of 4.17% (for residents of Hawaii)	_____
	Shipping and handling ($3.50 for book or kit, plus $3.00 each for orders of 2 or more)	_____

Total amount enclosed _____

Please photocopy this order form, fill it out, and mail it, together with your name, address, and personal check or money order, to:

STARMEN PRESS
PO Box 698
Kilauea, HI 96754
808-828-2166
starman@aloha.net
www.starmen.com